MONEY SMART

THE INDIAN WOMAN'S GUIDE TO MANAGING WEALTH

Reenita Malhotra Hora is a financial journalist and Ayurveda clinician based in Hong Kong. She anchors *Money for Nothing*, an award-winning live daily radio show about finance and investing. As a print journalist, she has contributed to *Reuters*, the *South China Morning Post*, the *Wall Street Journal*, *New York Times*, *CNN*, *Asian Investor*, *Times of India* and the *Economic Times*. She is the author of five books – *Inner Beauty*; *Ayurveda: The Ancient Medicine of India*; *Forever Young*; *Operation Mom*; and *When Arya Fell through the Fault*.

*

Divya Vij is Director of Operations Consulting at Acquisory India Consulting Private Limited, a firm that provides specialized services across mergers and acquisitions advisory, and operations and risk consulting. Prior to this she was Deputy Manager and Consultant with the Assurance and Business Advisory Services at PricewaterhouseCoopers, where she worked on statutory audit, management audit, internal audit, tax audit, PF trust audit and financial review. She lives in Noida with her husband, two children and three dogs.

Praise for *Money Smart*

'My role model for financial investing and strategy is my mother. As a child I would watch and learn how she managed the modest salary that my father received as a naval officer, ensuring that the household was perfectly managed, and yet managing to put aside small sums as savings that were invested wisely. From her I learnt important financial lessons: the power of compounding; the wisdom of investing in blue-chip shares and staying invested for the long term; that taxes and tax planning were an essential part of household budgeting.

In the course of time, as I interacted with the wonderful entrepreneurs whom I have had the privilege to work with as part of our micro-finance programme, I discovered that managing money wisely was a core competency of Indian women. Even with the tiniest sums of money, they managed to provide for their families' needs and still put a little bit away for a rainy day. Despite this, most Indian women, when asked, will say that they don't understand finance and will leave the major financial decisions to the men in their lives – often with sub-optimal consequences.

I hope that *Money Smart* will give every Indian woman the confidence and impetus that she can and must plan for her wider life horizon.'

– **Meera Sanyal**
Former CEO and Chairman, Royal Bank of Scotland in India

'Fortunately, our retail financial markets are deepening, offering consumers a wide variety of products and transaction channels. This needs to be accompanied by the capability to make appropriate financial choices. Unfortunately, there is no formula for taking the "right financial decision" or a quick answer as to which product to pick – it is necessary to acquire the knowledge to be able to make the right choices, given an individual's circumstances. These choices can extend to selection of the right financial institution, the right products or even choosing the right advisor. The choices change over time, requiring course correction. Irrespective of whether women are earners themselves, or support other family earners with their homemaking roles, women need to manage money, not only for their own but also their families' financial prosperity and security.

Unfortunately, many women consider "managing money", the activity essential to achieving economic prosperity, to be a stressful task. If you want to get the stress out of anything, first get "the unknown factor" out of it – the feeling that I don't understand it and therefore I can't do it. A book like *Money Smart* will remove the stress from managing money. It will be a map-reading guide – to give women the confidence and the tools to navigate their own journey to financial independence and security.'

– **Veena Mankar**
Founder, Swadhaar Group

'It is important as an informed citizen to know the status of the economy and what direction the finances of the country will take. Along with the big picture, it is equally important for women to know what is going to affect their everyday lives and the returns on their investments as well as their household budgets. Women should also know their legal and economic rights and look for specific schemes or tax incentives being announced for women.

In the past, Indian women wisely invested in gold – and look at what a large fortune or savings they have in their households. There weren't that many alternatives those days and women were less exposed to alternate investments... Today, with so many alternatives available for investment, the Indian woman needs to understand the various alternatives available to her, the yields available on each, and the implications...so that she can decide what suits her requirements best based on the stage of financial cycle she is in and also based on how sophisticated an investor she has become. A book like *Money Smart* will give women more knowledge of the choices available to them.'

– **Lalita D. Gupte**
Non-executive Chairperson, ICICI Venture Funds Management Co. Ltd, and Chairperson, India Infradebt Limited

MONEY SMART

THE INDIAN WOMAN'S GUIDE TO MANAGING WEALTH

REENITA MALHOTRA HORA
DIVYA VIJ

hachette
INDIA

First published in 2015 by Hachette India
(Registered name: Hachette Book Publishing India Pvt. Ltd)
An Hachette UK company
www.hachetteindia.com

SRD

Book illustrations by Mistunee Chowdhury

ISBN 978-93-5009-888-2

Hachette Book Publishing India Pvt. Ltd
4th & 5th Floors, Corporate Centre
Plot No. 94, Sector 44, Gurugram 122003, India

Typeset in Minion Pro 10.5/14.7 by
Manmohan Kumar, New Delhi

Printed and bound in India by
Manipal Technologies Limited, Manipal

FSC www.fsc.org
MIX
Paper | Supporting responsible forestry
FSC™ C043100

For

Pushpa and Gopal Krishan Vij.

our dearest grandparents who always encouraged us to lead with knowledge

Contents

Planning your portfolio: Making wealth your long-term companion

Illiquid Investments: Investing outside the box

Globalizing your portfolio: Why stay local when you can go global?

Taxes: Relax, it's just tax!

The Union Budget and you: Decoding the Budget

Foreword

TO EARN MONEY, I WOULD ENCOURAGE EVERY WOMAN TO realize what she loves doing and where her skills lie. There is no better way of earning money than by doing the things you love. It's not the choice of career that decides your income; it's your belief in your ability to offer something unique that makes all the difference. If you don't see the value in what you are doing, the world won't either!

I would like to emphasize that while financial goals are important, don't let them overwhelm you. Don't pursue financial goals at the cost of other things that matter to you, and only do what you are comfortable doing.

Financial independence means so much more than just getting a pay cheque. It is about earning the money you deserve, and spending, saving and investing it wisely, thus enabling you to realize your ambitions. The right guidance and education can transform your life as well as the lives of those around you.

Financial independence is not a chore and you can enjoy a comfortable life while managing your money. In order to optimize the money in your pocket, think about your objectives and how you want to achieve them. Educate yourself about the financial markets and examine the options available to you so that you know the best way to invest your money. If the process seems daunting, Reenita and Divya's *Money Smart* is here to help you take those initial steps.

As a banker with four decades of experience, I have never been more optimistic about the Indian economy as I am today. This book caters to the Indian woman who is investing in the Indian market, offering her a range of solutions to better manage her money and get great returns over time. Take advantage of it to build your life and fulfil your dreams.

Kalpana Morparia
Listed among *Fortune*'s 50 most powerful women in international business

Introduction

INITIALLY, I NEVER THOUGHT THAT MY COUSIN DIVYA AND I WOULD write a book about personal finance. As a financial journalist who anchors a daily radio show on the markets, the economy and investing, I always took it for granted that everyone loves money. After all, my mornings at the radio station were characterized by listeners calling in to ask our experts for tips and advice on how to get the maximum bang for their buck. For the longest time, I thought my show's listenership represented the world at large. I was to realize later how naïve I was.

Several months into the show, I began to wonder why such few women called in. It didn't make any sense; all the women I have ever known – friends, family and colleagues – have all had an eternal love affair with cash. The fact that it flew in and out of their purses made me think that these women controlled their stash of cash. So why weren't they calling in to ask for investing tips like their male counterparts? Weren't they interested in growing their stash to either be prepared for an unknown contingency or spend on bigger-ticket items?

Clearly not.

As I thought about it over time, I realized two things. Firstly, everyone *is* interested in money but more so in *spending* it than *saving* it. Secondly, when it comes to investing, there are a lot of people out there who are clueless (with a capital C). The mention of 'finance' scares the pants off many people. For them, it's something to desperately avoid. In fact, it is like walking alone in the dark.

At first, I thought it was just women who fit this peculiar demographic. I remember interviewing Mrs Moneypenny who writes a column in the weekend edition of the *Financial Times*. Appalled by how much women shy away from the subject of finance, she insisted that every woman needs to know something about money and investing. I agreed with her completely and decided to investigate this further with my cousin, Divya, a well-respected tax and audit consultant in New Delhi. 'Is it true?' I asked. 'Do Indian women really consider finance the dreaded F-word?'

'Women all too often rely on their husbands or someone else to control the finances,' Divya said, confirming my doubts. 'It works for many, but what if you suddenly find yourself in the driver's seat, responsible for making all the decisions?' She was absolutely right. And, it's not just women! Yes, it's true that a large portion of the investor audience comprises men but there are plenty of men who are equally scared of the F-word – they just don't greet it with the same gusto that they would cricket or beer. This is problematic, considering finance is the underlying thread that weaves together the fabric of every household.

That's when it occurred to me that Divya and I needed to get together to write this book – as a service to womankind in India. To alleviate the fear of the F-word by proving how simple and efficient it can be to take control of your personal finances and to invest your money so that you have a chance to grow your wealth. And to make sure that you never have to walk in the dark ever again.

It all begins with a simple question – how do you manage your money?

There's no denying that money is essential for just about every aspect of living – daily sustenance, education, healthcare, entertainment. But it's also a great asset, something that can be saved for a rainy day, and if invested prudently you can maximize it over time to splurge on bigger and better things.

Though managing your money seems like a no-brainer, many people simply end up spending more than they had bargained for on a one-time purchase. It's not like we are trashing the idea of retail therapy. Don't get me wrong – there are times when retail therapy might just be what the doctor ordered. But this is profitable only if it is meted out in small and measured doses. Going overboard can have a dire impact on other areas of your life – your higher education, running your household, your children's education, emergency funds, purchasing a house or essential renovation, old age or disability allowances. Most of us don't realize it but managing your expenses is the first step you have to take towards becoming a better money-manager.

Even if you are not an earning member of your family, handing over the power of the purse to your spouse is never a good idea. As Divya often advises her clients, if nothing else, you need to understand how much your spouse earns, how much you have for yourself and how much money the family actually needs to spend or to save. So whether you are a wage-earner or a homemaker responsible for day-to-day budgeting in the household, think about how you can manage your finances, invest and grow the kitty.

This book is a short, sweet and uncomplicated guide to personal finance and investing. It will help you with the ins and outs of growing and managing your money in a way that won't bog you down with indecipherable jargon. Additionally, we've explored the concepts of financial markets, stock exchanges, the global financial crisis and much more, telling you why they are important and how you can make them work for you.

Think of this as a handbook or a pocket guide that you can refer to over and over, whenever in doubt. Before you know it, investing will become second nature and then you'll be wondering why it took you so long to get started in the first place! If there is just one takeaway that you should get from reading the book, it is this: managing and growing your money isn't rocket science. In fact, it can be as much fun as spending. Once you try your hand at it, chances are you'll be hooked!

Reenita Malhotra Hora
Anchor, *Money for Nothing* on RTHK Radio 3,
Hong Kong's top finance and investment programme

Savings

WHY YOU NEED TO STASH YOUR CASH

'It is a stark reality that the Indian woman does not have authority or power as an economic head of the household. All her money-related or finance-related decisions are made by someone else, mostly by a male member of the family, on her behalf. It is imperative to educate women to inculcate a savings habit in them.'

– **Usha Ananthasubramanian**
Chairman and Managing Director,
Bharatiya Mahila Bank

STEP 1

Why save?

MANASI WAS THRILLED WITH THE IDEA OF MOVING TO MUMBAI. After spending 22 years in Solapur, the allure of the bright lights and big city was just about all the invitation she needed to kick-start her adult life as a trainee in one of Mumbai's leading banks. Of course, junior employees aren't exactly paid big bucks and because Manasi had no relatives in Mumbai she set up accommodation as a paying guest.

A few months in, Manasi had become quite comfortable with the reality of living in Dadar with Geeta Chopra, a woman who had been widowed 10 years ago. Manasi soon got busy with managing her life – she'd go to and come from work, and go out with her colleagues from time to time. Her pay cheque came through each month and she paid her rent on time – everything seemed just fine. But when she looked at her landlady, she couldn't help but notice how efficiently Geeta managed a whole lot of tasks without even a crease on her forehead. Geeta appeared to glide through life with remarkable ease, paying bills, dealing with tax issues, meeting with her investment advisor, planning trips to visit her children abroad – quite an overwhelming set of tasks from the point of view of her young paying guest.

'*It wasn't always like this*,' Geeta smiled when Manasi asked her how she could possibly manage so much with such efficiency. '*In fact, I was fairly naïve when I first arrived in Mumbai as a young bride many years ago. And throughout my life, my husband took care of everything. But when he died I was left to fend for myself. The day you find yourself on your own, you have no choice but to figure things out for yourself. I just wish I had started when I was younger.*

'*The only reason I'd ever had to step into a bank was to take my jewellery or return it to my locker*,' she told Manasi. '*All of a sudden I had to think about what I earned, what I spent, how much I needed to manage the household, and how much I'd need to save to get my daughter married. When you haven't as much as written a cheque before, the adjustment can blow your mind.*'

It's not that women don't have a propensity towards saving, or that they are not part of the financial decision-making in many households. But in a majority of Indian families, as it was for Geeta, the husband (in the case of an unmarried woman this would be her father or brother) is often the sole earning member of the family. In such cases, the women don't even have a clue as to how much money is being earned, let alone where and how the money is being invested for the future or for use in an emergency. In fact, contrary to popular opinion, such ignorance is rampant even among educated women living in India's biggest cities! Even in households where women earn, the practice is to hand over all their earnings to their husbands, or whoever is responsible for managing the finances.

Mindsets and cultural constraints often make it easy for us to forget that whatever the source of the earning, it is after all an income for the entire family. Every member of the family therefore has the right to decide how to spend or invest it. It will also not be very far from the truth to say that a majority of women believe that money and its management is a 'male' domain, that they will not be able to make sound financial decisions for themselves and their families, and that this area of decision-making should be left entirely to their fathers, brothers or husbands, as the case may be.

That said, life has a way of surprising you sometimes and not all of it is pleasant. Moreover, what are you earning for if not to enjoy every aspect of your life?

It is time then for you to recognize, and for us to emphasize, that regardless of whether you are married or single, whether you are earning or not, you must always be aware of the earnings, expenses, savings and financial planning being done for your family. Understanding how much money is coming into the household, how bank accounts are being operated, how and where the money is being invested, what insurance policies are at hand to cover contingencies is, therefore, critical. It's not a matter of being nosy, pushy or aggressive, but if you are to become truly financially responsible and independent, then this is the first step. Gathering more knowledge will automatically enhance your confidence and effective decision-making will then only be one step away. As we've mentioned earlier (and we'll keep repeating this often enough), none of this is difficult or overwhelming. It's just a matter of starting out and keeping at it until managing your money is that one habit you just can't give up!

Which brings us to the very first step you need to take – understand the importance of saving. The bottom line is this –

whether you earn your own cash, or whether someone else earns it for you, it's a good idea to put some away for a rainy day, because you know that old cliché: when it rains it pours. And when it pours, you have to be ready, we say! Saving money is critical, and not just for women like Geeta who might find themselves in a difficult situation one day. Truth be told, when you save, you are not just saving for life's rainy days but also for the fun, 'quality of life' moments that are so meaningful. One day you might want to finance your children's higher education, purchase a house or a car, or simply a piece of furniture, go on a long-cherished dream vacation, or even splurge on a piece of art. Saving your money *now* gives you the opportunity to spend it later on something that you truly want.

You may recall a television advertisement that was aired in 2013–14. Its message was so powerful it never ought to have been taken off air! A girl agrees to marry the boy chosen for her, but in 3 years time. '*Why the delay?*' the family wants to know. '*Because in 3 years, I'll have earned enough to have my own car and house on EMIs* (Equated Monthly Instalments, or the monthly payments you make towards a loan you have taken out) *and I'll go into this as an equal,*' the girl says.

That's it! Your savings are your protection and strength all rolled into one!

Saving vs Spending: Here's how you do it!

This chapter examines the nuts and bolts of how we women spend our money and how we can build savings. To begin with, let's compare savings with expenditure. You want to make sure that you can reserve a portion of the money at hand for emergencies and, at the same time, spread your income for lighter, more indulgent times throughout your life rather than restrict those. So how do you make sure that you can set aside enough money for savings and still have fun?

It's simple. First, draw up a checklist of all your income and expenditure items. Here's a sample of what this might look like.

MONTHLY INCOME CHECKLIST

1. Salary or business income =
2. Investment income (from fixed deposits, stocks, bonds, mutual funds, etc.) =
3. Pension =
4. Gifts* =
5. Property income (from rent or sale) =
6. Business income =
7. Inheritance income** =

Gross Monthly Income (A summation of all of the above) =

* You might not receive **gifts** on a monthly basis but it's a good idea to plan for monetary gifts that might come your way on birthdays, anniversaries or other significant dates.

** **Inheritance income** is also not typically a monthly receipt but it's good to factor it in especially as you grow older.

MONTHLY EXPENDITURE CHECKLIST

1. Food and groceries =
2. Rent or mortgage payments =
3. Loans (home loans, car loans, educational loans) =
4. Education (your own or your children's) =
5. Travel/commuting expenses =
6. Home maintenance (gas, utilities, repairs, etc.) =
7. Salaries (for domestic help) =
8. Taxes* (income tax, etc.) =

9. Entertainment (movies, eating out, guests, miscellaneous shopping) =
10. Doctor's bills, medicines =
11. Child care/Care for elders =
12. Minimum investment amount set aside for miscellaneous spends** =

Monthly Expenditure (A summation of all of the above)

* **Taxes** should ideally be planned for and paid monthly or quarterly in order to avoid a large one-time payment and possible interests or penalties. If you receive a salary, your company will automatically deduct tax at source from your salary.

** We recommend that you set aside a portion of your income as a part of monthly outflow, every month, for **investment** purposes.

Now, to calculate your ***net monthly income***, or what you are finally left with in hand, simply subtract the monthly expenditure from the gross monthly income:

GROSS MONTHLY INCOME - MONTHLY EXPENDITURE = NET MONTHLY INCOME

Now's when you can factor in the fun!

But first, before you decide on a ***fun budget*** for your more indulgent spends, you must set aside 25% of your net monthly income for savings.

It is important to set aside the savings amount before you calculate your 'fun budget' because you don't want to run the risk of having so much fun that there is nothing left over as savings at the end of the month!

The 'fun budget' should ideally be 75% of your net monthly income after expenses.

Now let's talk money.

If:

Gross monthly income	= ₹50,000
Monthly expenditure	= ₹32,000
Net monthly income	= ₹18,000
Ideal savings (at 25% of the net monthly income)	= ₹4,500
Then your ***fun budget***	= ₹13,500

Why do this?

Because:

- This practise will help you create the discipline to invest.
- If you make this a habit, it will help you sail smoothly towards financial independence.

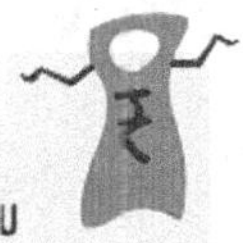

> More money means more options in life, whether you spend it on fun, charities or higher education.

- What's great is that any savings over and above this can be further invested.

STEP 2

Where should you hold your savings?

REMEMBER YOUR GRANDMOTHER USED TO TUCK HER MONEY under the pillow? Well, she could, because it was probably easier back then to trust that someone would not steal your cash.

You might think that stashing your cash in a safe place is the best bet. Alas, as great as this might seem for safeguarding your jewellery and keeping it out of the reach of a lurking thief, it certainly won't help your money grow. Now that you have understood the logic behind saving a portion of your income each month, the next things to consider are where and how to save it. Actually, the options available to you are fairly limited – you are either looking at a ***bank*** or at something called a ***Public Provident Fund*** (***PPF***). There are other vehicles that can be used to hold your money and make it grow but these fall in the category of investment vehicles rather than savings. We will discuss these in detail in the next section.

Your best bet is to park your money in a savings account in a bank or post office.

A bank account gives you a place to hold your money and also helps it grow slightly. How this works is fairly basic. A bank is essentially a financial institution that holds your money and then lends it out to others in order to make a profit. *What? Lend your money to others*, you will ask, *to make a profit?* Well, before you start losing your marbles, you should understand why this is a good idea. The fairly simple act of a bank taking your money and then lending it out to other people facilitates the flow of money to those who need it for investment and other productive needs, such as buying a house or a car, or borrowing funds to start a business.

At no time is the amount that you put in the bank at any risk, irrespective of what the bank does further with it. In return for holding your money there, the bank pays you a certain rate of interest. It follows then, that the longer your deposit term the more interest you will accumulate. Depending upon what kind of account you hold with your bank, you'll get a different rate of interest.

You need not have any doubts about the authenticity of this whole process, for banks are accredited financial institutions that operate under strict controls governed by the Reserve Bank of India (RBI), our country's central bank and financial watchdog.

A savings account typically gives a minimal interest of 3–4% but a fixed deposit can possibly give you a return of up to 8–9%.

Why banks are a good option:

- They make every aspect of your financial operations easier by issuing cheques and debit cards that allow you to make payments directly out of your bank account.
- They give you credit in the form of credit cards and also provide safe deposit boxes for you to store important documents and jewellery.
- They provide ATM (automated teller machine) services so you can easily access your cash from just about any corner of the country at any time.
- They even provide online banking services, enabling you to transfer funds to different parts of the country or the world at the click of a button.

STEP 3

Choosing an account type

NOW THAT WE HAVE ESTABLISHED THAT BANKS ARE THE SAFEST places to save your income, we will focus on the various types of accounts available and their suitability to your particular needs.

Which is the best account type for you?

Traditionally, there are two types of deposit accounts available in India. The first category is the ***basic bank account***, which can be a ***savings account*** or a ***current account***. The other category is the ***investment deposit account***, which is actually an investment in the form of a bank deposit. This includes the ***fixed deposit account*** and the ***recurring deposit account***.

Current Accounts

These are generally held by corporate entities and trusts rather than regular folks like us. However, if you have a business or are an aspiring businesswoman, this is what you need to know about current accounts: they are not intended for investment or savings. The purpose of these accounts is to park your money for a short period to enable you to facilitate transactions.

- Such accounts are highly ***liquid***, meaning that you can move your cash in and out smoothly at any time.
- Except for a few, most banks do not pay interest on current accounts. But they do impose a service charge to cover the administrative cost of transactions.
- The limits placed on the number of transactions or the amount of a single transaction in a day, and other accounts features, depend upon the minimum balance that you maintain in the account. For example, a balance of ₹50,000 may invite charges on transferring money above a certain amount in a day, or on issuing a demand draft exceeding a certain amount in a month.

Savings Accounts

Unlike a current account, which is used expressly by corporate customers, a savings account is used by individuals to hold on to their money and enable their savings to grow.

- A savings account will pay you a certain rate of interest, but still provide quite a bit of flexibility for transactions with cheques and debit cards.
- Up until 2011, the RBI fixed the interest rate on savings accounts at 4% of the daily balance. Since then, however, banks have been free to set their own interest rates as long as they abide by certain conditions imposed by the RBI.
- However, bear in mind that bank interest rates keep changing. Also, they are largely dependent on how much

money you have in the bank. For example, a bank might give 3% if you maintain a balance less than ₹50,000, but it might give you 6% if your balance is higher. It might also charge a penalty for lower balances.

- Most banks have rules for the maximum number of withdrawals and amount per withdrawal in a given period. In reality, though, not all banks enforce these rules as long as you visit the bank's branch to withdraw directly from your account. Even so, some of these rules are enforced for ATM transactions.

Fixed Deposit Accounts

If you have a large sum of money that you are looking to park then you'll want to consider a fixed deposit (FD). Since FDs are offered by banks, they are considered to be very safe investments. An FD is a financial instrument that provides you with a higher rate of interest than a regular savings account. The interest rate for FDs differs from bank to bank, and private sector and foreign banks generally offer higher rates of interest.

- The 'fixed' part of the deposit refers to its tenure. In other words, you agree to hold it with the bank for a fixed period of time or a fixed term. So fixed deposits are also sometimes known as ***term deposits***.
- The tenure of an FD can be flexible, ranging from a week to 10 years. For FDs of a 6-month duration or higher, the interest is typically compounded on a quarterly basis.
- Some banks have variable-interest fixed deposits, where the interest rates go up if market interest rates rise and come down if the market rates fall. Interest rates for FDs currently range between 7% and 11%, with higher rates offered to senior citizens.

- Your FD is typically paid to you as a lump sum on the date of maturity or the interest can be credited to your savings account at the end of every quarter. If you'd like it to be paid even more frequently, say every month, then the bank can do so but it will usually discount the rate.
- Some banks offer additional services to FD holders, such as loans against FD certificates at competitive interest rates.
- If the interest paid to a customer exceeds ₹10,000 in a financial year, then the bank automatically deducts a tax. This is known as ***Tax Deducted at Source (TDS)***.

Recurring Deposit Accounts

If you do not have a large lump sum to deposit in a bank but would like to put away a small amount every month and receive a higher rate of interest than a regular savings account, you should consider a recurring deposit (RD). These are special kinds of term deposits that make it easy for you to deposit a fixed amount every month and earn interest at the same rate applicable to FDs. Think of it this way – with an RD, you are effectively making FDs of a certain smaller amount in monthly instalments. This is how an RD works. Basically, you determine how much money you want to deposit into your FD each month (the minimum can be as low as ₹500 or ₹1000 but the maximum can be whatever you like, although some banks like to put a limit on this). The RD is then linked to your savings account and the bank withdraws your fixed amount on a fixed date of the month from your savings account and deposits it into your RD account.

- Normally, RDs are given for maturities ranging from 6 to 120 months.
- The bank gives you either a passbook, or paper or electronic

statements, allowing you to make entries for your deposits and the interest you earn. They also indicate the maturity value of your RD based on the assumption that the monthly instalments are paid regularly on due dates.

- Some banks also offer flexible RDs, allowing you to deposit even higher instalment amounts. If you find yourself needing cash for any sudden requirement or emergency, you can withdraw your amount prematurely – however, in that situation, you may end up paying a penalty. The bank may also make adjustments to the interest payable to you.
- The interest income earned in RDs is not exempt from tax. Tax is deducted at source on crossing the limit for exempted interest income. However, senior citizens often get extra benefits in the form of higher interest rates.

KEY POINTS TO REMEMBER

- While choosing your bank consider how easy it will be for you to get cash. Make sure your bank has a local branch nearby since certain transactions need to be done in your own local branch.
- The bank should have ATMs which are widely available. Also check whether there are any extra charges for using them.
- Before selecting any bank to open your account, see what special facilities they offer. For instance, will the bank pick up cheques and offer cash delivery at your home?
- Always remember your signature in the bank – in fact, keep a sample at home. Banks are very finicky about correct signatures. The slightest deviation or change in signature style can trigger a problem at the bank

- If you open a joint savings account, you need to specify whether this means you will be signing either jointly or 'either or survivor'. The former means that both account holders need to sign every cheque, while the latter has more flexibility, given that only one signature is required.
- In the case of joint accounts, it is advisable that both account holders sign on the cheques or transact at the bank so that both know the processes involved.
- Most banks have a system of sending alerts for any transaction in your account, so make sure to give them your contact details so that you can keep a check on unauthorized transactions.
- Whichever type of account you hold, specify a nominee. In the absence of a nominee, should anything happen to either you, or both account holders in the case of a joint account, it will be more difficult for your legal heirs to access the funds. In a single account the nominee will have direct access to the funds, whereas in the case of a joint account your co-account holder will automatically become the sole operator of the account and must specify a nominee.

Mixing it up: the magic of hybrid accounts

If you think that these accounts are not able to meet your banking needs, then worry not, for there are certain hybrid accounts available which provide additional benefits like high liquidity combined with high interest rates on savings. In order to meet these customer demands, banks now offer even more flexibility by combining features of two or more types of deposit accounts. Such accounts have different names at different banks, for example, 2-in-1 deposits, flexible FDs, savings-plus deposits, sweep-in deposits and so on.

The most common hybrid accounts are as follows:

- ***Flexible FDs***, which are linked to your savings account. If at any point you need to withdraw more than you have in savings, the bank automatically breaks your FD and transfers the amount to your savings account. The balance left in your FD will continue to earn interest at the original rate.
- ***Sweep-in deposit schemes***, which are particularly useful as they offer the high interest rates of an FD coupled with the liquidity of a savings account.

The sweep-in facility links your deposits to your savings account. You predetermine an upper limit for your savings account knowing full well, of course, that as you add income from gifts and salaries, the total amount in your savings account could exceed that limit. When this happens, the bank will automatically put this amount into an FD.

However, if you, at any time, find that you have insufficient funds to clear a cheque, the bank will automatically break units of the deposit to clear the cheque. The amount you withdraw will earn interest up to the date of the withdrawal at the rates applicable for the time the money was in the bank. The rest of your deposit will continue to earn the original high rate of interest. It is also possible for the bank to allow a sum of money determined by you to be re-transferred from your FD to your savings account.

Most people prefer sweep-in facilities because of the flexibility they provide. Sweep-in instructions need to be given to your bank at your branch or mentioned online.

Review the bank's charts to see the interest rates for different periods, to make the best possible decision; sometimes rates for periods spanning from 6 months to a year are the same. In that case, you don't need to block your amount for a year if you are getting the same rate of interest for a shorter period of 6 months.

The best way to find out which bank offers the best fixed deposit scheme is to actually study the details of their schemes and see for yourself.

It would be worthwhile to note that although bank deposits have historically been very popular due to their low risk, capital guarantee and relative liquidity, the fact is they cannot typically beat inflation and are not generally tax-friendly. Some banks also offer to maximize your returns by offering investment services through a ***demat account*** or an ***investment account*** that specializes in investment and growth. We'll elaborate on investment services in Section 3 of this book.

MONEYSMART ALERT!

TDS does not apply only to your salary and other income. It applies to your bank deposits, too. All interest earned on deposits, whether fixed, recurring or sweep-in, are taxable according to limits specified by the Income Tax Act. Banks are required to deduct TDS on deposits if the total interest earned on all your fixed deposits in a bank is more than ₹10,000 per financial year. Your bank will check whether your account is tax-exempt. If it isn't, then TDS will be deducted even on interest that has accrued but not yet been paid.

Your Money Mantra

Today, banks provide a variety of options suited to individual needs. It is all about finding out what works best for you.

- If you have a business and need to make frequent transactions, then you will need a current account.
- If you have a large sum of money that you do not need to dip into for a while, then you should consider a fixed deposit scheme to lock in a higher interest rate for the long term.
- Are you good at keeping records of maturity dates of your FDs and RDs? If not, then auto-renewal facilities are a good option for your accounts.
- If you prefer to keep most of your cash in either savings or current accounts, yet want full liquidity, then consider a 2-in-1 deposit, a smart deposit or a sweep-in deposit.

STEP 4

Choosing the right bank

LET'S NOW MOVE ON TO WHAT KIND OF BANK YOU SHOULD choose to save and invest in. You must make an informed choice, since you are going to trust this bank with your hard-earned money.

WHAT THE EXPERTS SAY

'For women in the traditional Indian patriarchal set-up, developing a relationship with a bank can provide them with a range of products and services that will help them achieve financial independence. Functional banking relationships, besides providing the benefits of transactional banking, also provide a comprehensive range of solutions that assist in asset and wealth creation, financial planning and education and retirement planning...and give women...control [over] savings of the family.'

– **Naina Lal Kidwai**
Group General Manager and Country Head, HSBC India

India's banking sector is made up of four types of banks: ***nationalized banks, state banks, private-sector banks*** and a number of ***foreign banks.***

There was a time when private-sector banks were growing at a faster rate than nationalized banks. Today, nationalized banks, which were considered slow and bureaucratic for the longest time, have become far more efficient. In fact, some private-sector banks, too, can be quite cumbersome to deal with due to the endless paperwork and fact-checking required under the RBI-mandated Know Your Customer (KYC) procedures.

When you are considering whom to bank with, it is worth noting that no single bank is necessarily better than another. Today, all banks have access to online banking facilities, a vast network of ATMs and branches, and interbank services.

If you are a working woman, the decision of which bank and branch to open an account with normally rests with your employer since they would probably open your salary account with a bank with which the company has a corporate current account. Companies do this to make it easier for them to transfer salaries each month. Having said that, you can have more than one account – one for your salary and one for other income – provided you can maintain both or more of them. (Salary accounts typically do not insist on a minimum balance, but other types of savings accounts could require ₹1,500 to ₹25,000 to even ₹1,00,000 as minimum balance to be maintained. These norms vary from bank to bank.)

Then again, your situation might be totally different. For instance, you may need to develop a banking relationship for a business. In that case, you'll obviously need more flexibility in determining where to open your account.

MICROFINANCE AND MICROCREDIT: RURAL BANKING FOR WOMEN

Microfinance is a matter of great importance as it is considered a key method for empowering women in rural India.

Although there is a massive migration of the Indian population to urban areas, women who live in rural India need financing to run small-scale industries to keep them going. These women rely on financing or small amounts of money lent to them at a low rate of interest so they can develop their businesses.

Historically, India's rural women have depended on private moneylenders for micro-financing, which has only led to severe exploitation. Today, new microfinance and microcredit options are available that offer them a safer, non-exploitative path. A wide array of loans are now being offered by a range of providers such as specialized microfinance institutions (MFIs), nationalized banks like Allahabad Bank, Bank of Baroda and Union Bank of India, and even private-sector commercial banks like HSBC, Axis Bank and Kotak Mahindra Bank.

HSBC, for instance, lends to microfinance institutions. It also helps them in running training programmes to help their members learn financial skills to run a business, learn a trade or become an entrepreneur, enabling them to repay their loans and begin to save earlier in the business cycle.

WHAT THE EXPERTS SAY

What is the difference between planning for your livelihood (be it employment, a small business or anything else) if you are a rural vs an urban citizen?

'The biggest difference between rural and urban citizens is access to banks and financial advice. In high-inflation environments like India, inflation reduces your real savings, further highlighting the importance of investing well. Additionally, with greater integration, connectivity and migration between rural and urban populations, people's aspirations in rural areas are significantly changing. To counter inflation more effectively and match one's increasing aspirations, it becomes important to increase the level of savings.

Microfinance has provided much-needed loans to the poor who have no collateral to offer and who otherwise go to moneylenders who charge very high interest rates. This borrowing can be to fund care for illnesses, schooling or a ceremony.

The most exciting use of microfinance is where the woman has used this to start a business – be it embroidering or tailoring or rearing chickens or vending vegetables. I have seen how quickly she begins to save money while meeting her loan commitments and indeed grows her business. Her voice in family decisions improves and she begins to take charge of investment and spending. Microfinance has largely been a rural phenomenon because of the self-help group (SHG) model, although this is now seeing some success in urban experiments as well.'

– **Naina Lal Kidwai**

Group General Manager and Country Head, HSBC India

Which is the best bank for women?

Every bank has its pluses and minuses, and each of you has unique needs. Your research to see which bank and its schemes will work best for you will have to be thorough.

That said, there are some banks in the country that offer special services for women and so it's worth highlighting those.

Allahabad Bank

The oldest joint-stock bank in the country, its ***Mahila Sanchay*** account is specially planned to attract and empower women in society.

Andhra Bank

This bank has worked hard for the empowerment of women and has designed under its agriculture business segment specific schemes for women. They have established SHGs to supply micro-credit to rural women with their emergent needs.

HDFC

This bank offers complete solutions for women, catering to their banking, investment, insurance and lifestyle needs.

South Indian Bank

South Indian Bank (SIB) has launched a savings bank account exclusively for women called ***SIB: MAHILA***. This packaged savings bank product is linked with an RD, with one year 'house-to-house' travel insurance and accidental death insurance cover.

State Bank of Mysore

The bank offers some interesting schemes specifically for women, including the ***Gagan Mitra*** personal loan for air hostess training and the ***Stree Shakti*** package for female entrepreneurs.

State Bank of Travancore

The State Bank of Travancore (SBT) has two products specially designed for women, a savings deposits scheme called ***SBT Prathibha***, and one for young girls named ***SBT Sukanya***.

UCO Bank

The bank offers collateral-free loans called ***Mahila Shilpa Udyog***, with interest concession for female entrepreneurs.

Vijaya Bank

Primarily a farmer's bank, it offers financial loans to women in non-farm development economic activities through its ***'Assistance to Rural Women in Non-Farm Development' (ARWIND)*** scheme as well as its ***'Assistance for Marketing of Non-Farm Products of Rural Women' (MAHIMA)*** scheme. The bank has always helped rural women by providing loans on the lowest interest rates.

Bhartiya Mahila Bank

Most exciting of the lot, perhaps, is India's first women's bank. Opened in 2013, the main objective of this bank is to empower women through financial inclusion. Although the bank accepts deposits from everyone, it lends mostly to women. Still fairly new, the bank plans to open 500 branches all over the country by 2017, including villages where women face more problems opening accounts. The bank offers women-centric products that other lenders don't offer, such as funding for a catering business, for opening day-care centres and for kitchen upgrades.

WHAT THE EXPERTS SAY

'There are banks with a history of over 100 years. They also cater to the needs of women. But banks that cater specifically to the needs of women are more empathetic to women customers and they also motivate and inspire them to take up economic activities. Such banks are continuously inventing some product or the other for the welfare of Indian women. Tailor-made, special lending programmes are also available. So it is indeed critical for the Indian woman to bank not just with any bank but with such banks that would benefit her in the long run.'

– Usha Ananthasubramanian

Chairman and Managing Director, Bharatiya Mahila Bank

Your Money Mantra

Deciding which bank to do business with and what type of account to open is the first step in your journey towards financial independence. Taking these decisions will not only put you in charge of your own money, but also give you the confidence to move out of your comfort zone and explore other avenues, like investing.

- Research and identify a bank that offers women-centric products suited to your lifestyle as a student, entrepreneur, working professional or homemaker.
- Remember that one bank is not necessarily better than another. It's all about identifying the one with facilities that suit you and make it easy to carry out online and offline transactions.

STEP 5

Looking the other way: alternate saving schemes

IF YOU NEED TO PARK SOME IDLE MONEY, IT'S WELL WORTH realizing that banks are not the only option available to you. The truth is that most women will veer towards banks because, as mentioned earlier, they are regulated by the RBI.

That's not a bad thing, but you must not limit your options. ***Non-banking financial (NBF)*** institutions help grow your money often at higher rates of return than most banks.

Take a look at some of these options:

Employees' Provident Fund (EPF)

This is a compulsory contribution scheme intended to promote savings among people with lower income. The government mandates business enterprises with more than 20 people on their payroll to provide provident funds to their employees. Essentially what happens is that the employer deducts a certain amount from the employee's salary account for the fund and also contributes an equivalent amount to it.

For monthly earnings of ₹6,500 or less, both employee and employer are required to contribute (this may be optional, in which case, only the employer needs to contribute) to the EPF at the rate of 12% of expenses, amounting to basic wages, dearness and retaining allowances, if any. Once you earn above ₹6,500, your participation in the EPF scheme becomes voluntary. The EPF rules have changed, effective 1 September 2014, to cover anyone with a base salary of ₹15,000 (an increase from ₹6,500 that was applicable earlier).

- You can withdraw from the EPF as an advance, or take a loan against it based on some terms and conditions which are further based on whether the EPF trust is private or not, and then go as per company rules.
- If you change your job, your EPF is simply transferred over to your new company through the use of your Universal Account Number (UAN). If you are not going to get any further EPF deducted, you can even withdraw the amount.
- Non-resident Indians (NRIs) cannot contribute to EPF. It is only applicable to employees working in India, for an Indian company.
- The Employees' Provident Fund Organization (EPFO)

and the central government fix the interest rate for EPFs each year. Currently it has been set at 8.75%.

- The interest income from the EPF is tax deductable. However, if you withdraw before completing 5 years of service, you will forfeit your tax benefits. Additionally, there are restrictions for withdrawals prior to 15 years: you can withdraw only a certain percentage every year until the 15-year lock-in period is over.

In case you are looking for a job change, the best way out would be to transfer the EPF to your new company rather than withdraw it. This proves more beneficial in the long run and also saves you from paying taxes for the premature withdrawal.

Public Provident Fund (PPF)

In PPFs, you are permitted to make voluntary contributions ranging from a minimum of ₹500 to ₹1,50,000 or above annually. There is no cap on the maximum amount you are allowed to contribute to your PPF, but tax exemption under Section 80C is given only up to ₹1,50,000. Here, too, you are entitled to a tax write-off for all income earned. However, your money is locked in for a period of 15 years. NRIs are not eligible for PPFs. The Government of India decides the rate of interest for PPF accounts. The current interest rate, effective from 1 April 2013, is 8.7% per annum.

Technically speaking, there is little difference between EPFs and PPFs. The former is employer- or salary-driven, while and the latter happens at your own will. Given a good interest rate and tax benefits, the basic rule is that if you don't need the money, let your PPF balance grow. Of course, some of this depends on you and your funds requirement at a given point in time but ideally you should try and make this the last resort for funds withdrawal.

In fact, opening a PPF account is a great savings option for women with children or dependants. You can claim tax exemption under Section 80C in your tax return while putting this money away for your child every year. However, the tax deduction cannot exceed the limit specified in the Income Tax Act.

Imagine the amount that will be accumulated based on your yearly contributions once your child reaches college-going age! A minimum contribution of ₹500 is all that's required to keep this going, if you find that in certain years you are unable to contribute more.

Remember, a company contributes to the EPF and not to a PPF. Both contributions can be made simultaneously each year, but the tax break is taken jointly for both up to the defined limit for the year.

Post Office Savings

Post Office Savings offer small, risk-free savings instruments that promise steady returns. Guaranteed by the government, they are considered to be very safe with zero default risk and a slew of tax benefits. If you do the math, you might find that on an after-tax basis the returns on these schemes could be higher than those available on bank deposits.

The various post office saving schemes available are:

Post Office Time Deposit

Just like FDs in banks, Post Office Time Deposits (POTDs) are for those who want to deposit a lump sum for a fixed period. The annual interest rate for a POTD ranges from 8.4% to 8.5%. The minimum investment is ₹200 with no prescribed upper limit, and the deposit time-frame ranges from 1 to 5 years.

Post Office Recurring Deposit Account (PORDA)

These are similar to a bank RD, in that you can invest a fixed amount on a monthly basis for a fixed tenure of 5 years. A PORD account offers an annual fixed rate of interest of 8.4%. The minimum investment in a PORDA is ₹10 and there is no prescribed upper limit as long as you invest in multiples of ₹5.

National Savings Certificate (NSC)

NSCs are an assured return scheme with numerous tax benefits. The annual interest rate for NSCs is about 8%. A deposit of up to ₹1,00,000 qualifies for a tax rebate and there is no TDS.

Post Office Monthly Income Scheme

The Post Office Monthly Income Scheme (POMIS) is ideal if you are looking to make a regular monthly income. It can be opened with a minimum initial investment of ₹1,500 or later on with multiples of this amount. It can be opened either jointly or as a single account. However, there are different limits prescribed for each scenario. A single account can hold up to ₹4.50 lakh, whereas in case of a joint account the prescribed limit is ₹9 lakh.

The interest rate is 8.5% per annum which is payable monthly and the maturity period is 5 years. You are also allowed to close the account prematurely.

Company Fixed Deposit (CFD)

CFDs are fixed deposits that are similar to banks. This particular kind of investment may not be as widespread nowadays, though some companies might still offer such deposits.

CFDs also earn a fixed rate of return over a period of time but, unlike banks companies are not backed by the central government, making them less safe than bank deposits. It is important that you realize that the CFDs are not a very secure option – if the company defaults you cannot sell the company to recover your capital investment. Therefore, make your decision wisely.

If you want to invest in a company, its credit ratings become very relevant, not merely to understand the stability and reputation of the company but also in terms of understanding how much interest you will receive. Higher rated companies offer lower rates of interest, and vice-versa.

Your Money Mantra

Once you start saving and handling money yourself (irrespective of whether you are working or whether your spouse is the earning member in the family), you will realize that there is a lot that you can do with your money. You can make your money work for you instead of you working for it.

- Opening a bank account allows you to have a functional relationship with the bank, which will further motivate you to try new products.
- Exploring alternative saving vehicles is a great idea as it gives you the scope to maximize your interest income.

Growing your money

MAKING YOUR MONEY WORK FOR YOU

'If you look at the life patterns of women, you'll see that they tend to live longer than men but that their careers are interrupted by family needs. More often than not, women prefer a conservative investment strategy. Given inflation and the many responsibilities they have taken on, as well as the high aspirations they have, there is a compelling need for women to take charge of their financial planning.'

– **Suresh Soni**

CEO, Deutsche Asset Management India Pvt. Ltd

STEP 1

The power of investing

IF FINANCIAL LITERACY IS AT THE TOP OF YOUR AGENDA – AS IT should be for all Indian women – then one of the first things you have to do is to get rid of the fear of the word 'investing'. Although it may seem daunting at first, once you have a basic idea as to how investing works, you'll see that it is anything but difficult.

In this chapter, we will explore investing as an option that can help you grow your money into much more than it is worth today.

Investing: a smart strategy

Gauri Kothari was just 19 years old when she knew she wanted to get a master's degree. '*It was a tall order,*' she recalls. '*I come from a very traditional family where education is not really a priority for girls. With some difficulty, I started a bachelor's degree programme but my parents were very keen to get me married as soon as possible. I knew that the only way I could break out of the trap was by becoming financially independent.*'

Gauri managed to find herself a job as a management trainee in a hotel soon after she graduated. A regular salary was one step towards financial freedom but she was a long way off from being able to afford a postgraduate education.

'*For five years, I scraped together everything I could in savings and then invested it. It was the only way I could think of to make my money grow. I wanted to put my money in the capital markets but I couldn't afford a financial advisor so I read everything I possibly could about investing in mutual funds and equities. I was intrigued by the idea of investing my money in equities because they seemed to offer a fairly high return but I was also scared of the idea of losing my money if the markets went down,*' she recalls.

Growing up, Gauri believed that the only way to earn an income was by getting a job. She wasn't wrong, but while she wanted more money, she didn't want to work more hours. In this situation, investing seemed like the smart thing to do. Eventually, after quite a bit of research and advice from finance-savvy friends, Gauri decided that the best way for her to make more money was by accessing the capital markets though hybrid mutual funds. Still, it took her three years of saving, investing and a bit of gift money to come up with sufficient funds for her master's programme.

GOLDEN WORDS FROM THE GLOBAL GURU OF INVESTING

WARREN BUFFET

If there is anyone in the world who is the most qualified to define investing, it's Warren Buffet, the Sage of Omaha, who really is the global guru of investing. Here's his definition for investing, taken from his company Berkshire Hathaway's 2011 letter to shareholders.[1]

'Investing is often described as the process of laying out money now in the expectation of receiving more money in the future. More succinctly, investing is foregoing consumption now in order to have the ability to consume more at a later date.'

Buffett's definition actually describes everything that an average Indian woman wants do with her money. For all intents and purposes, this means making her money grow so as to reap profitable returns. But now the question is, how does she invest this money?

Investing in the right kind of asset is a strategic decision that gets better with understanding and practice. But here again, Buffet's sage council comes to our rescue. He talks about three major categories of assets.

The first category includes investments that are denominated in a given currency, such as money-market funds, bonds, mortgages, bank deposits and other instruments. Buffett says that most of these currency-based investments are thought of as 'safe' but in truth they are among the most dangerous of assets because their value fluctuates with time.

The second major category of investments involves assets that are not productive but are purchased by the buyer in the hope that someone else will pay more for them in the future. He cites the example of tulips, which briefly became a favourite of such buyers in the 17th century.

The third type of investment that he talks about requires an expanding pool of buyers, who, in turn, are enticed because they believe the buying pool will expand still further. Owners of such productive assets are not inspired by what the asset itself can produce but rather by the belief that others will desire it even more avidly in the future, and hence there will always be a possibility to sell it at a profit.

Buffett's own preference is to invest in the third category.[2] His company routinely invests in productive assets, such as businesses, farms and real estate because he believes that others will desire these in the future. You will do well keep this principle in mind whenever you make any decision regarding investing your money.

The basics of investing

Investing certainly is the key to building wealth but investing without planning is not a good idea. If you want your money to grow, you have to invest wisely. There are some things that any woman interested in investing must keep in mind at all times.

Patience is the key

There is no such thing as a get-rich-quick scheme. Like everything else, you'll need to be patient and go through some good days and some not-so-good days and, yes, the learning curve can be steep. But one thing is for sure: the rewards will far outweigh the effort you put in.

Risk is a necessary evil

There is, of course, always a certain amount of risk involved with putting money into the markets and there are no guarantees, but investing is more than merely counting on luck. Investing wisely means spending time and energy to learn the tools of the trade so you can do a thorough analysis. Investing is all about making an informed decision about putting your money into those avenues where you can expect a reasonable profit and simultaneously manage the risk involved.

Put yourself in charge

Taking control of your personal finances is the ultimate step to financial freedom and security. It's great to have banks and investment professionals around to help and advise you, but why let them make decisions regarding your cash?

Ultimately, you know what is best for you and your money.

What is the difference between saving and investing?

Without doubt, they overlap. As we learnt in the previous section, a savings account is a place to hold your money while you earn a small amount of interest on it. However, this interest doesn't constitute a solid return. So is this a waste of time?

Not at all.

Every little bit of interest helps and a bank account is a safe place to park your money, but remember that one of the things we experience every day is inflation. Even with a good savings habit, the interest you earn might not be enough to cover inflated costs over the course of time.

> A good investment strategy is future-oriented; you need to evaluate your options by keeping in mind the assets which will be popular in the long run.

You might be wondering then, why bother with an entire section on savings rather than going directly to investing. Relax – one of the biggest mistakes we make in our quest to grow our wealth is to risk putting the cart before the horse. It's practically impossible for anyone to invest without actually having saved some money first. Take, for example, an investment tool like bonds, which most people buy in order to preserve their capital and then grow it. If you didn't have savings, you wouldn't have any capital to invest!

So now that you actually have some money saved up, the big question is, 'What do I invest it in to increase the value of my money?'

Your financial advisor might talk to you about investing in financial instruments such as fixed income instruments (for example, ***bonds***) and equity (***company stocks***). Your friend might be convinced that buying a piece of contemporary art is a great investment, whereas your father might tell you to look no further than real estate.

Essentially, all of these are different assets that you can invest in – stocks, bonds, art, property, etc. But how do you determine which instrument is best for you? Do you go by what makes sense (but how do you determine that?), what is most fun or what is guaranteed to give you the highest return?

In the following chapters, we will discuss various investment options in detail so that you can choose the ones that suit you best.

STEP 2

Which financial assets should you invest in?

ALTHOUGH THERE ARE DIFFERENT KINDS OF FINANCIAL instruments that you can invest in, we are going to look broadly at securities, or assets that can be traded (such as stocks and bonds), and those that cannot (such as real estate). Generally speaking, there are four traditional categories of assets that can be invested in:

Debt Securities

A debt security is an investment vehicle that provides you the opportunity to lend your money to a company or to the government for a fixed period of time. In return, the company or government will pay you interest. Hence, it is also known as a fixed income asset. And because the company is in debt to you, it is also known as a 'debt security'. Eventually, the company or government will pay you back the amount you lent them.

- Debt securities include bank notes, government and company bonds, and company debentures.
- Government bonds are commonly accessible through the capital markets.

Equity Securities

Equity securities or stocks essentially give you the opportunity to purchase a share of a particular company. This entitles you to vote at a shareholders' meeting of that company and allows you to receive any profits that the company decides to distribute to its shareholders. These profits are known as ***dividends***.

- When we talk about equities, we refer to the stocks of publicly listed companies which are open to purchase by the lay investor through the capital markets.
- Sometimes, investors are able to purchase private equity or stocks of private companies that have not yet gone public but this is not as common and not possible through the general capital markets.

The Dutch East India Company was one of the first modern joint stock companies. It actually issued stocks that paid dividends on all the proceeds from all the voyages that the company undertook, rather than on a single voyage.

Mutual Funds

A mutual fund is essentially a collection of stocks and bonds. When you buy a mutual fund, you join a group of other investors, all of whom have pooled their money to pay a professional fund manager to select and manage a specific basket of debt and equity securities on their behalf.

These managers put together funds based on a specific investment strategy. They might choose to focus on large stocks or small stocks, governments bonds or company bonds, developed markets in the West or emerging markets in Asia, specific industry sectors and so on.

- What's good about a mutual fund is that it offers you the ability to diversify your investment in both stocks and bonds without going through the time, effort or paperwork required to invest in a single stock or bond.
- Paying a professional to do the research and manage the investment might ensure better returns in the long run.
- However, you should try to know as much about them as you possibly can before choosing to invest in them. Do not hesitate to do your independent research and discuss the options with your advisor before making any decisions.

Alternative Investments

Aside from the two basic categories of securities – debt and equity – there are also a number of other alternative investment vehicles. These are more complicated types of securities such as ***derivatives***, or securities that are derived from equity and debt. Derivatives include financial instruments known as forwards, futures, options and swaps. These require more complicated investment strategies for advanced investors, so we won't really discuss them in this book.

Alternative investments also include investing in assets, such as foreign exchange, gold and property. Although, traditionally, gold and property are considered to be ***hard assets***, or assets that you can see, touch and feel, as opposed to than ***paper assets***, like bonds, stocks and mutual funds.

In recent years, companies have essentially securitized these hard assets allowing you to invest in and trade them as ***securities***. This essentially enables you to own a piece of gold or a portion of real estate on paper, though, for instance, you do not actually have the gold in your bank locker. The advantage of gold and real estate securities is that, unlike their hard assets, paper assets are more liquid and easier to trade.

Your Money Mantra

Be clear on what your risk appetite is and always balance your portfolio between risky and non-risky investments. Don't be taken in by the promise of high returns.

- Consider carefully what kind of asset you want to invest in, whether it is a hard asset or a paper asset. The advantage of the latter is that it can be liquidated more easily.
- Even if you employ a fund manager or an investment advisor, make sure you are always kept in the loop while decisions are being made.
- Be patient. While investing in any asset you should be aware that your money can remain tied up for a longer term, but this is the best way to reap its benefits.

STEP 3

Investing in non-traditional assets

MANAGING YOUR PERSONAL FINANCES IS REALLY ABOUT managing your life. There are certain areas of your life that you must invest in, even though they might not seem very lucrative. These investment options are quite different from the traditional avenues that we discussed in the previous chapter, mostly because they do not yield any returns, not in the traditional sense of the word.

The option that we are holding up for discussion in this chapter is ***insurance***.

These are investments you make for a rainy day, in the event that things go wrong. Because expenses related to health, accidents, hospitalization and so on can add up to huge amounts at a time, it is best to prepare for such exigencies in advance.

Insurance comes in various forms: ***health insurance*** (which includes medical insurance, a subset of which is accident insurance, and critical illness insurance), ***life insurance*** and ***general insurance*** (which covers a variety of areas such as motor vehicle insurance, home insurance and even unemployment insurance).

The best time to take steps to protect your future is the present, in case you haven't already done so.

WHAT THE EXPERTS SAY

'There are three kinds of insurance that women must buy.

First, medical insurance that pays hospitalization costs: In a metro, a health cover worth 10 lakh is a must. Second, term insurance that covers about 10 years of annual income: If you are a homemaker, insurers will restrict the amount of cover because you do not have an annual income. In that case, buy a stand-alone accidental death insurance plan. Third, a critical illness policy: A few insurers cover critical illnesses specific to women, for example, breast, uterine and ovarian cancers.

These are good plans to buy.'

– **Kapil Mehta**

Managing Director, Secure Now Insurance Broker Pvt. Ltd

Health Insurance

Unlike our ancestors, it is not likely that we are going to live for a hundred years.[3] With the increased health risks posed by urbanization and modern lifestyles, it is likely that you might be in need of healthcare at some point in your life. Investing in a health insurance policy is then a must for every woman.

But before we move on, be forewarned that this is not an investment that will give you a return. Neither do you earn any income from it nor can you encash it at any time. Rather, it is an insurance policy against a future medical expenditure.

Indian women account for 15% of the global burden of heart disease, which kills about 15 million people every year,[4] and the World Health Organization (WHO) has said that one in every 12 women in urban India will develop cancer.[5]

Investing in a medical policy can help you cover the risk of healthcare should you require it in the future. If you are employed, you should check whether your company offers a corporate health insurance policy, in which your company would pay for the premium as well as the covers.

What's nice about these is that they provide cover not only for you but also for your spouse, kids and even your dependants.

While medical policies cover the expenses of hospitalization, they have certain conditions.

- If you first apply for a medical policy, it will not cover pre-existing diseases. Generally, you would have to wait for a period of three years to cover existing conditions.
- Usually, personal mediclaim policies don't provide cover for any pre-existing diseases and pregnancy. However, the mediclaim provided by companies to their employees have better terms, and they usually cover most of this. Insurance plans covering maternity are still in their nascent stage in India.

- Medical policies generally become more expensive as you age and your health worsens. So the best time to buy a health insurance plan is when you are still in good physical condition.

Types of Health Insurance

There are two broad categories of health insurance: ***medical insurance*** (which includes accident insurance) and ***critical illness insurance***.

Medical Insurance

This provides hospitalization cover and pays medical costs for diseases or surgery should you be admitted in a healthcare facility. Also, accident insurance, which insures you against the risk of accidents, is worth considering if you have a hectic life that requires you to constantly be on the move. Again, you should be aware that this is not an income-generating investment.

In fact, we also suggest that you take out medical insurance for all those on your payroll – domestic staff, drivers, anyone else who works for you – as this will prevent you from shelling out huge sums of money for hospital fees, should there ever be need for it.

Usually, companies are required to provide liability insurance to cover the cost of accidents that their employees might meet with on the job. But remember, it may be better to have a personal policy on the side, even if your employer has a mediclaim cover for you and your family.

Critical Illness Insurance

This provides cover against the threat of major ailments, but doesn't cover ordinary hospitalization and medical expenses.

Critical illness insurance does not have any maturity value. The insurance company pays a pre-determined lump sum if you are diagnosed with a critical illness that you have determined in the initial contract.

Some critical illnesses to include in your policy

- Organ transplant
- Cancer
- Multiple sclerosis
- Coronary artery bypass surgery
- Paralysis
- Heart attack
- Kidney failure
- Stroke

The payment is typically effected within a few days of the diagnosis and once made, the policy ceases to operate. The amount of cover might lapse if not used. However, the terms and conditions of each plan could differ and have to be taken into consideration along with the plan.

For information on various leading health insurance providers and the best policies provided by them, please refer to Appendix 1a on p. 294.

Life Insurance

Life insurance is essentially an agreement between you and the insurer, in which the latter agrees to pay a specified sum to your beneficiaries when you pass away, or to you at the end of the term period. Although they are called 'life' insurance policies, in actuality, they typically provide coverage for a long period rather than the policy-holder's entire life, say for a maximum of 30 years, or up to a certain age. The major benefit of having a life insurance policy is the mental peace you derive from the knowledge that in your absence your near and dear ones will be taken care of. It's an important insurance, especially for single women with dependants. You need not invest in a life insurance policy if you don't have a family or any dependants.

- Life insurance policies offer the additional benefit of allowing the policy holder to take loans against them. You don't need to worry about repaying the loan as the amount will automatically be deducted from the total amount that you will receive on maturation of your policy.
- They also offer tax benefits and can be helpful in dealing with liabilities.
- All insurers have different permutations and combinations. Some life insurance policies also provide medical facilities. In some cases, you can get a certain payback, for example, after four years you may get 40% back, or the payback could be linked to your retirement (hence the term 'retirement benefit insurance policies').

Types of Life Insurance

Life insurance plans are broadly categorized as ***protection-based policies*** and ***investment-based policies***.

Protection-based Policies

These are created to provide cover if and when an event happens. In this kind of policy, the payment is made in the form of a lump sum and the most common example of this is ***term insurance***.

Investment-based Policies

Investment-based insurance plans such as ULIPs (Unit Linked Insurance Plans) are products that give you the benefits of insurance as well as investment in a single integrated plan. Typically, this means that a part of the premium is used to pay for the insurance cover, while the rest is invested into debt and equity securities. In these plans, the premium can be paid at regular intervals or all at once.

This poses the question – which one is a better option? Let's see what our experts have to say about this.

WHAT THE EXPERTS SAY

Traditional life insurance vs unit-linked policies: Which is better and why?

'Traditional insurance gives lower long-term returns, but it is also less volatile than unit-linked insurance. Traditional insurances award annual bonuses based on performance of the insurer's general fund. By law, this is primarily invested in government bonds. On the other hand, unit-linked policies are market-linked. They allow an investor to get access to equity markets.

Due to this, returns can be higher but also more uncertain. If you are below 50 years of age and can take a long-term plan of over 10 years, then purchasing a unit-linked policy will be a better and more cost-effective option for you. However, if you are over 50 and want returns over a short period then traditional insurance is more suitable for you.'

– **Kapil Mehta**

Managing Director, Secure Now Insurance Broker Pvt. Ltd

Model your life insurance plan according to your individual needs

If you are going to buy a life insurance plan, then you also have to determine its cover size. Life insurance is meant to provide your dependants with enough money to replace your income in case of your untimely death. You have to make sure that your life insurance takes care of things like basic family expenditure, major expenses like your children's education loans and their marriage expenses. In order to do that, you need to ask yourself questions like, are you the sole earning member of your family or are there multiple members who can apply for life insurance? Or are there any other alternative sources of income available?

Generally, your life insurance should cover about 10 years of your annual income.

Above all, what you don't want to do is underinsure yourself – if your life insurance cover is inadequate, then you might as well not have any insurance at all.

It's worth getting insurance with a long term and large cover. The key is to start out as young as possible. Often, insurance companies will offer you a shorter term policy – one that expires in, say, 10 or 15 years – but with a much lower premium than, say, a policy that lasts 20 or 30 years. It can be tempting to go for this since the premium is so much lower than that of long term policies but the costs may not benefit you in the long term.

Of course, this is just one of the factors that affect your premium. A variety of other parameters are taken into account by the insurance company when calculating your insurance premium. These include age, with different premiums being offered for different age groups, status of your physical health, the term of the policy and your income.

Different Forms of Life Insurance Policies[6]

Term Insurance

This is a life insurance plan for a specific term, usually valid for a maximum of 35 years.

Group Life Insurance

As the name suggests, this is meant for groups rather than individuals like employers or associations wherein more people are covered. Every insurer has his own terms and conditions, like age bracket, number of people required for the group policy, and so on.

Senior Life Insurance

This is a general life insurance and not specifically 'Senior Life Insurance', as the term indicates. The differentiating factor is that not all insurers offer life insurance to individuals over a certain age and, if at all they do, it is usually at a much higher premium.

Whole Life Plans

These have no fixed maturity dates and the payment is made to the beneficiaries upon death of the insured party.

Unit-linked Insurance Plans

These are combinations of life insurance and equity- or debt-oriented mutual funds.

Endowment Plans

These are combinations of an investment and term-life insurance designed to provide an assured sum of money on the expiry of the policy.

Pension Plans

These cater to stability in the future, and are generally meant for old age. Every plan will have its own features. Normally, you pay the premium as per the schedule which could be for 5, 10 or 20 years, and then after a certain period, you start receiving a regular sum every month or every quarter which continues throughout your life, just like a pension.

Money-back Policies

These are policies in which you are paid a portion of the assured sum periodically and the entire sum is paid to your beneficiaries upon your death.

Child Plans

These are combinations of insurance and investment which cater to parents who want to plan for their children's future.

MONEYSMART ALERT!

Many financial planners agree that a term plan is the best kind of life insurance as it offers a substantially high cover at a low price. The premium of a term plan is very small compared to that of an endowment plan, a money-back policy or a unit-linked policy that offer the same coverage. Part of the reason for this is that, unlike the others, there is no investment component in a term plan and the entire premium is dedicated to covering the risk.

General Insurance

Although the greatest part of general insurance is health insurance, it also includes other forms of insurance such as homeowners' insurance and automobile policies. As in the case of health insurance, general insurance will not give you a return but it is a good thing to have in reserve for unforeseen incidents. Here are some forms of insurance that come under the umbrella of general insurance.

Home Insurance Policies

These secure your home against fire, theft and other natural calamities.

Motor Vehicle Insurance Plans

These cover expenses for repairing or replacing a vehicle damaged in an accident.

Travel Insurance

It covers costs related to cancellation, theft or other travel-related situations like delayed flights.

Theft and Burglary Insurance

Though the terms might seem similar, there is a fine line of distinction between theft and burglary. The former results from outside interference: for example, if a factory has a break-in and assets get stolen. The latter covers the damages incurred from an inside job: for example, someone like a guard of the factory commits burglary. Whether you get your claim or not depends on the kind of crime you're a victim of. These specifics are outlined in the insurance paperwork, but most people do not read the fine print. Always ensure you read the paperwork carefully.

You can refer to appendices 1a and 1b for a list of life insurance and general insurance providers.

WHAT THE EXPERTS SAY

'Even if you work with an advisor or agent, do make sure that they share all the details with you before you buy insurance.

I would consider these four factors while buying any insurance:

The claims payment track record of the insurer: This is available in IRDA's annual report and in the public disclosures that insurers make every quarter. Make sure your insurer has a good record.

Exclusions and conditions of the insurance: This is best assessed by reading the policy thoroughly. Too often, people read the policy contract only after purchasing insurance. In fact, this should be done before you even consider buying the policy.

Price should be low: There can be large variations for the same insured risk. For example, health insurance plans can vary by as much as 50% with no material benefit changes. Always compare prices.

Renewability and lapse conditions of the insurance: You should have the flexibility to revoke an insurance plan without paying any penal costs. Also the insurance should be renewable for as long as you wish without any arbitrary increase in price.'

– Kapil Mehta

Managing Director, Secure Now Insurance Broker Pvt. Ltd

KEY POINTS TO REMEMBER

- There are situations when public-sector insurers may be better and others when insurers from the private sector are more efficient. Similarly, stand-alone health insurers are good for some products but sometimes the larger general insurers can be more competitive.
- Ideally, work with an advisor who can provide comparisons. Compare the different features and prices of all the insurance options available to you to select the plan that suits you best.
- Are you working with an insurance broker or an insurance agent? The former is independent and therefore likely to give you better advice than the latter, who represents a company.
- You should be very careful while assessing a recommendation. Generally, agents will recommend products from which they earn more. In life insurance, the highest agent earnings tend to be traditional insurances, followed by unit-linked insurance. Term insurance and single premium products generally have the lowest earnings.
- Try and get the insurance done through an insurance broker because brokers help facilitate cashless insurance and claims that may get stuck for any reason later on.
- Also check which third party agent (TPA) is being used by the insurance company. The TPA needs to be good at smoothly clearing claims or facilitating cashless hospitalization.
- Do your research thoroughly – does your medical plan cover the cost of medicines, tests, hospitalization and doctor visits?

- Are you entitled to tax benefits? You should be, particularly in the case of critical illness. Premium on both mediclaim policies and life insurance plans enjoy exemption under sections 80C and 80D of the Income Tax Act, subject to certain limits.

Your Money Mantra

Insurance is your safety net, a good option for investment. Like other investment options, insurance is also future-oriented – it is something that we invest in for a rainy day. With a wide array of choices available, these points will help you take the right decision.

- When investing in a life insurance policy, start young and go for as long a term as possible.
- Your health and age are factors that will be taken into account when you go to buy a medical insurance. Try and maintain a healthy lifestyle in order to avoid high premiums.
- Read the fine print and clarify the terms and conditions so that you are fully aware of the scenarios in which you are sure to get the insured sum as well as the situations that are not covered under the plan.

STEP 4

Understanding your investor profile

BY NOW YOU MAY BE WONDERING WHAT KIND OF ASSET IS THE best to invest in. Truth be told, they all have their pros and cons. For instance, debt securities are perhaps safer than stocks but stocks can possibly give you a higher return. Purchasing a home might not translate into easy cash but it will give you a place to live in and chances are that if you want to sell it in the future, the value will go up if the economy remains stable.

There are some things you should keep in mind before you chalk out an investment strategy:

Diversification

Since different securities perform differently over time, if you mix up the assets you invest in your entire portfolio will not suffer should any one particular kind of security decline in value. So, for example, if the value of your stocks goes down, you will still have the stability of the bonds in your portfolio.

This is called ***diversification*** and its basic mantra is, 'Don't put all your eggs in one basket.' If you spread your investments across various types of assets and markets, you reduce the risk of a catastrophic financial loss.

Individual Approach

You also need to consider how active or passive you would like your investment strategy to be because your unique approach in investing will differ accordingly.

With an ***active investment strategy*** your aim is to individually select securities that outperform the markets. So if you or your financial advisors are actively looking at a company's publicly available financial statements before investing in its stocks or bonds to determine whether it will do better than other companies in the financial ecosystem, then you are actively managing your portfolio.

A ***passive investment strategy***, on the other hand, means you are not aiming to outperform the markets but would rather invest in securities that track or mirror market performance. One example might be an index-based mutual fund that matches or tracks the components of the public capital markets index known as the Sensex (we'll talk more about the Sensex in Section 3).

Financial Goals and Risk Profile

Your investment portfolio should combine different investment assets put together for the purpose of achieving your financial goals. So, first, make a list of your financial goals. This might seem a little far-fetched, especially if you are young or if you have never done this before but we cannot stress enough that the sooner you plan for this, the better.

Your list could include the following:

- Building an emergency fund to take care of yourself in the event that you lose your job
- Financial security for yourself and your child/children
- Building funds to educate or pay for the marriage of your child/children
- Buying a home
- Life insurance
- Building a retirement fund

Once you have listed your financial goals, you can plan how to grow your wealth by investing in different asset classes to meet the above objectives.

Most often, if you work with a portfolio or investment manager, he or she will require you to fill out a detailed risk-profile questionnaire before suggesting what assets you should invest your money in.

Once you have answered the questions, your banker or investment advisor will calculate your risk score or, in other words, assess how aggressive an investor you are, and then suggest suitable investment products allocated per asset class to match your risk appetite and meet your goals.

He or she will also give you a monthly report showing you your portfolio as a pie-chart. The whole pie represents your investment and each portion of the pie represents a specific asset to which you have allocated a certain portion of your investment.

It's up to you to combine the assets in any way you like to meet your financial goals. The asset mix of your pie-chart will determine the risk you take and the return you can expect; in other words, the unique risk–return profile of your portfolio.

No two women have the exact same financial goals.

A 70-year-old widow living off her husband's retirement portfolio will be more interested in preserving the value of her investments than, say, a 30-year-old executive with a monthly pay cheque. The widow cannot risk losing her investments. She needs the income from them to pay her bills. The executive, on the other hand, can afford to be more aggressive by taking more risk in her investing strategies.

Divestment

Kenneth Andrade, Head – Investment, IDFC Asset Management, advises against divesting all your equity holdings in one go. Why? Because you can't predict what markets will be like in the future. If the markets hit a historic low the year you retire, you would significantly lose the value of your investments. To protect against this, Andrade advises a systematic divestment plan, just as advisors suggest a systematic investment plan. '*Since you have been putting money into your portfolio year-by-year, you also take it off the table year-by-year. The biggest mistake that people make is to just take their money out of equities in one shot. That can hurt you because it's a volatile asset and God forbid you take it all out at the wrong time. If, on the other hand, you reduce your portfolio by 10% a year over a period of five years before retirement, you can do much better. Why? Because equity is a cyclical asset, a three-year span gives you time to ride a complete cycle,*' he adds.

What is your investor profile: Aggressive or Conservative?

Do you have an aggressive investment strategy that aims for the highest possible return, or a conservative investment strategy which prioritizes the safety of your investment?

An ***aggressive*** investment strategy is typically appropriate for investors who have a high-risk tolerance. In other words, those investors who are able to deal with wide fluctuations in the values of their investments, with profits and losses, in order to get a higher return over a longer time period.

An aggressive portfolio is generally one that has a higher proportion invested in equities. Here's an example of a ***moderately aggressive*** portfolio. Half of it is invested in equities and the other half is split up between fixed income, cash and gold.

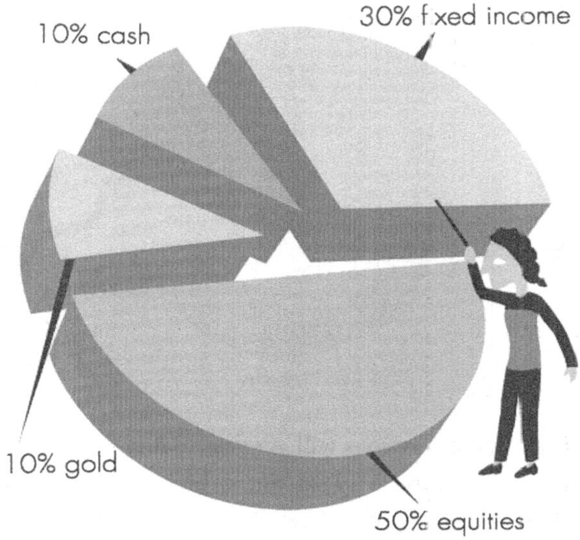

A ***conservative*** investment strategy, on the other hand, prioritizes the safety of your investment. This strategy is more appropriate for investors who are risk-averse – in other words, those who do not want to deal with losses and have earmarked a shorter time period for their investment.

The main goal of a conservative portfolio strategy is to protect the value of your rupees against inflation – at the very least, this is something we all should aim to achieve. A conservative portfolio strategy will generally consist of cash or high-quality fixed-income securities.

Here's an example of a conservative portfolio that is mostly invested in bonds but also has some long-term capital growth potential from equities.

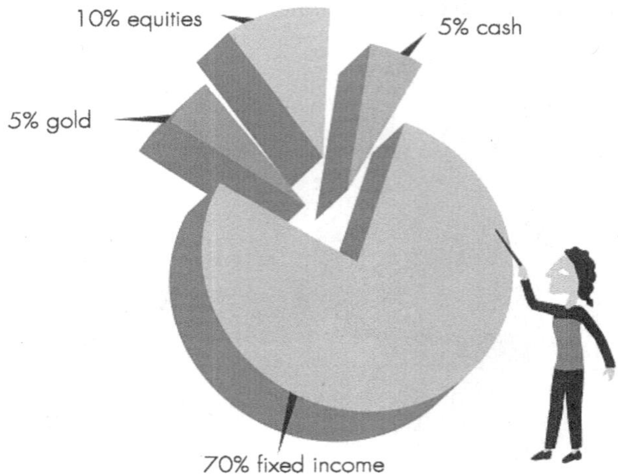

Most investment advisors will suggest that if you are starting young, then it's a good idea to put a higher portion of your portfolio in equities as you will have more time ahead of you and can naturally take more risk. The general thinking is that this will allow you to beat inflation over time and even give you the opportunity to encash some of your wealth to convert into a hard asset like a home, or to pay for an event like your child's wedding. Then, as you approach retirement, you basically convert the major portion of your equity holdings to debt.

Of course, everyone has a bit of a different take on this. Andrade says that at the outset it is a good idea to have a sizeable portion of your portfolio invested in assets that are linked to inflation – equities, gold and property – and the rest in assets that give you an annuity-like fixed income. '*I would think about my investments from an income point of view and a portfolio point of view. Set aside about 30% of your income each year for investment into equities – because this is a compounding asset. Over time, it will translate to about 45% of your portfolio,*' he says.

Your Money Mantra

Investment is an individual activity and it revolves around your unique circumstances. The following points are crucial to your investment plan.

- Invest in a variety of assets in keeping with your financial goals so as to minimize risk and maximize returns.
- Every woman has different investment needs complimenting her financial status and her stage of life.
- Have a proper divestment plan in place as a counter measure to inflation and market volatility.

STEP 5

Getting yourself a demat account

IN THE OLD DAYS, IF YOU BOUGHT COMPANY SHARES YOU would be issued a share certificate for the number of shares purchased. You would hold on to this evidence of your share ownership until you decided to sell your shares. Now, while it is always good to have physical proof of ownership of your assets, common sense will tell you that the downside of this is the risk of loss, theft, damage or forgery.

However, these days, investors have the ability to hold shares electronically rather than on paper. This conversion of physical records of your investments into electronic records is called the dematerializing of securities. Today, you can hold your securities electronically in a ***dematerialized or demat account*** rather than messing around with share certificates.

KEY POINTS TO REMEMBER

- You can open a demat account when you register with an investment broker.
- It can also be opened by a bank or a smaller investment advisor. The bank will generally open your demat account for free with your other accounts, but you should check this specifically with the broker.
- The advantage of going to a bank is that it provides comprehensive research about various products. However, you should know that bankers might push a lot of products your way just to make a commission.
- Your demat account number is quoted for all transactions facilitating the electronic settlement of all trades. You need an internet password and a transaction password to operate your demat account.
- You do not need a demat account to invest in mutual funds or sell units that you have purchased. Mutual funds are managed by financial institutions, which collect money directly from you. Of course, if you have an existing demat account, you can definitely use it to invest in mutual funds.

STEP 6

Your investment checklist

✓ Start early

Because the growth of your investment is based upon the mathematical concept of compounding, the earlier you start the more you will grow your wealth over time. To understand this better, consider this example.

Aarti invested ₹2,000 at the age of 25 at an interest rate of 8% that was compounded annually. By the time she turned 50, she had accumulated more than ₹6 lakh in her bank account. Compare this to Bina, who also invested ₹2,000 at the age of 35 at the same interest rate of 8%, which was also compounded annually. By the time she turned 50, she had around ₹4 lakh in her bank account. Aarti started investing earlier and she ended up with ₹2 lakh more in her bank than Bina. At the age of 60, Aarti would have even more in her account than Bina, all because she began investing her money 10 years before Bina did.

Of course, bear in mind that examples such as these work on the assumption that there are no outflows from their accounts and there is no change in interest rates.

Also, it might be better to start with the less risky investments first. Put some amount of your money in fixed deposits, where the principal does not get eroded and then set some aside for more risky investments.

✓ Understand risk

Investing is risky business. There is just no getting around that even if you try your best to curb it. So when someone tells you to invest in a government bond or a blue-chip stock because it is risk-free, do not fall for it.

Even the best of governments and companies can run into financial trouble – it is a situation that we've seen over and over again. The company could end up defaulting on a loan and as for a government, well, in theory, it can print more currency to repay its loan but printing currency generally leads to price inflation, so ultimately you will end up with lower returns on your investment. The chances of this happening are low but it's something you must be aware of at all times.

✓ Understand the company or fund that you invest in

When you invest your money, you should do your research. If you cannot understand something, keep at it till you do. Mutual fund managers are hired specifically by corporates and mutual fund companies to know the ins and outs of the funds they manage. Ask your investment agent or broker to explain the investment in clear, simple terms and not in typically complicated sales jargon. Research the company thoroughly before you decide to put even a single rupee into one of its stocks or bonds. Look for companies that are doing well, that have profits and growth potential.

WHAT THE EXPERTS SAY

'When you look at a company from the outside, there are any number of financial parameters that drive that company. If you can identify just one or two of those parameters, you can make an informed investment decision. What is the one thing that keeps the company ticking? Why, in a down cycle, when everyone is asking you to sell, should you re-look at investing in this particular company? If you have a reasonably good handle on statistics, research and analysis, then you can look at investing directly in company stocks; if not, then go for an equity mutual fund, where you hire a professional to do the work for you. But even then you should ask questions about the underlying stocks in the fund you have invested in.'

– **Kenneth Andrade**

Head – Investment, IDFC Asset Management

✓ Diversify your portfolio

Be disciplined about this. Do not put more than 10% of your entire portfolio into a single security, even if your financial advisor or your best friend tells you that it's the fastest way to prosperity. At the same time, be wary of holding too many stocks as you don't want a situation that is difficult to manage.

✓ Monitor your investments regularly

Investing is just the first step. Once you have begun, you don't want to sit back and let things happen by themselves. Keep in touch with the companies you have invested in by following them in the press. Look at the price updates on your portfolio sheet at least once a week. Assess whether your investment in a particular security was a good decision or not, and why. Learn from your past mistakes because there is no better way to learn than through first-hand experience.

✓ Do you need an investment specialist?

Investment Specialists are a dime-a-dozen these days.

Portfolio management services will create an investment portfolio for you based upon stocks, fixed income, debt, cash, structured products and other asset classes, all tailored to meet your individual requirements and managed by a professional manager. They charge management fees and usually take a small share of your profit, too. Could this be useful?

Perhaps it could be if you are a high net-worth individual and own very large sums of money, or if you would like to invest in equities and don't know how to. But if you have less than a crore to invest, you have to question whether it makes sense at all.

You could also choose to appoint an independent financial advisor who will analyse your financial goals, risk appetite and advise you on investment decisions accordingly.

These folks are usually qualified chartered accountants or certified financial analysts who work on a fixed-fee basis or a profit-sharing basis, but they do not sell financial products themselves. Again, this might be useful for you if you feel you are just not qualified to make financial decisions, or if you don't have the time to manage your own portfolio, or if you feel that it would be helpful to bounce ideas off of a professional.

KEY POINTS TO REMEMBER

- Make sure she or he has spent time in the business – at least 10 years. No Johnny-come-lately, please.
- Make sure that she or he is doing this full-time and not as an on-the-side gig to make an extra buck.
- Make sure that she or he is a licensed professional. Check credentials thoroughly; scam artists are aplenty.
- Make sure you ask for references; talking to other clients about this professional firm, about the experiences with them, will help you make the right decision.
- Make sure that you are in the driver's seat when it comes to actually making the investment. Take recommendations and advice from the right advisers but the authority to make a decision should rest with you.

STEP 7

FAQs for the first-time investor

INVESTING IS A DECISION THAT REQUIRES PLANNING. MANY first-time investors have major areas of concern that need to be addressed before they can make a commitment. Here we will address some of the frequently asked questions that every first-time investor asks – or should ask.

Q What kind of investments will ensure that my principal will not be eroded?

Investments in fixed income or debt securities are designed to keep your principal investment safe and grow it to protect against inflation. Purchasing a bond or a debt-based mutual fund is ideal if principal preservation is your goal. Mind you, in the case of mutual funds, be sure that they are entirely debt-based rather than hybrid (that is, with some proportion of equity).

Q What kind of returns can I expect from my investments?

Your returns depend entirely upon the interest generated from the assets you decide to invest in. When it comes to debt instruments, bank fixed deposits can earn up to 8% or 9.5%, while mutual funds can go up to 13–14%. The interest rates are determined entirely by the RBI and will fluctuate over time. In the case of investing in equities, the price of shares depends upon various factors, including the general economic conditions, how well the company is doing and what people think of it despite how well it is actually doing.

Q How can I predict the future of my investment and its appreciation, especially when it comes to gold and property?

The price of gold fluctuates daily, just as shares do. Keep a watch on this price and read as much as you can about the demand and supply of gold in the financial press.

Property prices vary with regard to the demand and supply of real estate in the particular location. Land has a tendency to rise in price in the long term because as development occurs, land becomes scarce. In cities, there might be fluctuations in prices of flats and sometimes there are market crashes, but in the long term property prices tend to rise. The price of flats may not really fall as such but the comparative appreciation is lower than that of land.

- Do your research on areas that have high demand. Property prices will often rise. There are plenty of property sites where you can check the rates online. These are generally listed by location and type (that is, whether they are commercial or residential).
- With all your assets, regardless of what type they are, resist the tendency to be 'wedded' to them. Every year, if not more frequently, you should assess whether it is worthwhile holding on to them or whether it is time to sell.
- Always remember to diligently check before investing, especially in property-related matters, to ensure that the papers are okay and there are no defaults.

Q Will I get any tax benefits from the investments?

There are plenty of assets that come with specific tax benefits. You also have the option of opting for investment-related financing that provides tax benefits. For example, if you apply for a home loan, you will receive a tax benefit while investing in a piece of property as long as you intend this to be your primary home.

Mutual funds are tax-exempt, as are dividends from fixed-income investments.

Before you invest in anything, check with your investment advisor and your tax consultant as to which investments have tax benefits.

Q Is investing outside the country an option for me?

You are allowed to invest up to the equivalent of US $250,000 in any currency in most countries without RBI approval. There are a few countries, like Pakistan, where you cannot invest without the government's approval, and Bhutan and Nepal, where you can invest only in Indian rupees. To do this, however, you will need to work with a broker outside the country or invest in global mutual funds.

Q Prices of essential commodities like petrol, vegetables and cooking gas, etc., are going up at an alarming rate. Will investing help me in planning for this?

Investing will certainly help as the basic aim of saving and investing is to grow your money to counter price inflation. We all know that prices of commodities are determined by the economics of supply and demand. Generally, when there is a scarcity of goods, their prices will rise. We see this periodically with food, cooking gas, etc. Creating a fiscal buffer through investment will certainly help you deal with this more easily.

Q Will currency fluctuations affect my investments?

If you are investing in Indian securities, then it should not make much of a difference. However, if you are investing in foreign funds, commodities, or any kind of investment denominated in currencies other than the rupee, then currency fluctuations will certainly affect your investments.

Planning your portfolio

MAKING WEALTH YOUR LONG-TERM COMPANION

'Investment is simple but not easy. The investor's chief problem, and perhaps her worst enemy, is likely to be herself. Investment-related biases and errors are agnostic to gender. Mutual funds make good investment sense, in particular to a woman investor for whom direct investment is not her cup of tea. Not only does direct investing require expertise, but it also requires constant monitoring and follow up.'

– **Leo Puri**

Managing Director, UTI Asset Management Company P. (Ltd)

STEP 1

The nuts and bolts of portfolio planning

NOW THAT WE'VE DISCUSSED INVESTING AND THE FACTORS THAT necessitate it in some detail, there is one more thing you should think about: Is your money lying idle?

Let's illustrate what we mean when we say that.

Consider Anjali Mittal, a 25-year-old media professional. Anjali saves ₹25,000 of her salary every month and invests it in so-called safe avenues like National Savings Certificates (NSC), Public Provident Fund (PPF) and life insurance policies offered by the Life Insurance Corporation (LIC).

It seems like a good idea, especially in light of what we've discussed in the previous sections. All three schemes – PPF, LIC and NSC – offer tax incentives.

> Investing is a very simple concept. All you have to do is identify how much you need, when you need it and how much you can spare. This is all you need to figure out your investment strategy.

Her friend, Ritika Bose has a slightly different story. She is an IT professional who saves around ₹30,000 each month – ₹10,000 of this goes into a bank RD, so her total investment comes to ₹1.2 lakh a year in the principal and, beyond that, she earns an interest of 8.5–8.75%, which will be computed on the basis of her monthly deposit per year. The remaining ₹20,000 remains idle in her bank account.

On the face of it, it doesn't look like they are wasting any money. After all, they have diligently assigned a portion of their monthly income to appropriate saving instruments.

The reality is a bit different. Given a decent enough rate of interest, they will have to pay tax on their interest income. Add to this the rate of inflation, which averaged around 7% in 2014. What this means is that, 10 or 20 years later, though their corpus would have grown, it wouldn't be enough to cover their expense given what the price of things in the market would be then. So in real terms they would have had a negative return on their investment.

Every woman needs to keep some amount of her monthly earnings in the bank or other liquid investments in order to cover day-to-day expenses and emergencies. However, in order to meet your long-term financial goals, you must think about building a solid investment portfolio that is composed of a variety of assets, some of which carry more risk and others less so.

But this is easier said than done. After all, how do you begin to think about building the right kind of investment portfolio?

Here are some questions that will provide a good start:

Himanshu Kohli, CEO of the investment advisory and management firm Client Associates, says that one of the first things you need to ask yourself is how much wealth you require for your sustenance.

'*Think about your objectives here given your earnings,*' he says. '*Are you happy to depend on your parents or your husband like many Indian women, or are you looking for complete financial independence? In other words, do you want to consciously survive on your own till the age of say 80 or 90, given the annual rate of inflation?*'

You also need to ask yourself whether you are already there. Have you achieved financial independence already? If not, then how long do you need to work to get there?

And then, what is the real rate of return your portfolio should target? According to Kohli, it is important to look at real returns on a post-tax and post-inflation basis rather than on absolute returns. '*If the current rate of inflation is 7% and you are invested in a fixed deposit that gives you 9%, you may think that you are doing okay. But on this you pay 30% tax so your net return is actually just 6%. In this case, you are getting a negative real rate of return.*'

Consider this scenario: Sakshi is a young woman in her 30s. Currently, her lifestyle is such that her monthly expenses are around ₹5 lakh. By the time she turns 55, her monthly expenses will have shot up to ₹27 lakh assuming that she hasn't made any changes to her lifestyle. In addition to this, she would like to get her child educated at a premier school. Today, those expenses come to ₹2.5 crore, but by the time her child actually goes for higher education, 16 years from now, those same expenses would be ₹7.3 crore. Similarly, if she has kept aside ₹3 crore for her child's wedding expenses today, in 20 years those expenses would have shot up to ₹11.6 crore.

Sakshi needs to consider what kind of returns she wants to generate on her investment portfolio.

At a return rate of 11%, she needs to invest ₹2 lakh to cover monthly expenses, ₹1.15 lakh per month to cover her child's education expenses and ₹1.02 lakh per month to cover the marriage expenses. This brings her total monthly investment expenses to ₹4.17 lakh per month.

However, if she waits for another 10 years and decides to start investing her money when she turns 40, then given the current rate of inflation of 7%, her real investment needs would be that much higher. She would need to invest ₹8.15 lakh to cover monthly expenses, ₹6.76 lakh for education, and ₹4.75 lakh for her child's marriage – bringing her total monthly investment to ₹19.66 lakh.

So what's the bottom line?

If Sakshi waits for another 10 years to invest, to cover exactly the same expenses, she would have to put in 4.5 times more money than what she would need to put in today. Starting sooner is obviously better as she has more years to plan. Also, she needs to look at the larger picture rather than concentrating on immediate returns.

Unfortunately, most women do not think in these terms. Realistically, it's good to be pragmatic as you plan for the future by being aware that returns can and will go up or down in the short term. Try to separate your emotions and, if possible, don't get hung up on the idea of returns – at least not in the short term. Investing wisely means transitioning your focus from being 'returns'-oriented to 'process'-oriented.

And remember, everything makes a difference. The more you earn, the more you save and the sooner you start saving. To illustrate this point, Kohli cites the example of a cricket match:

'If you want to win the series and you totally depend upon the batsmen, that's not going to help you; if you put too much pressure on the bowler, that's not good either; but if you also have team spirit and put equal weightage on all three – batting, bowling and team spirit – then you definitely have a better chance of success.'

WHAT THE EXPERTS SAY

Five tips to chalk out your investment strategy

1. Identify what you need in life:
   - What is your age?
   - How long do you want to work?
   - How much do your goals cost you in today's economy?
2. What are your surplus assets?
   - Don't look at the house you live in, or the jewellery you wear, or the car you drive, as these are assets for personal use.
   - Make a list of how much you have in property, bonds, equities, gold. Also look at your cash flow from the assets.
3. Think about the real rate of return that your portfolio should earn.
   - What should your portfolio earn on a post-tax basis?
   - Based upon this figure, calculate how much you should invest in each asset class.
4. Calculate how much you can save on a monthly basis.
5. Revisit your portfolio on a monthly basis.

– **Himanshu Kohli**
CEO, Client Associates

'Your four basic choices for investment are ***equity***, ***debt***, ***alternate investments*** and ***hybrid*** or ***balance investments***,' says Kohli. In this section, we will broadly discuss portfolio planning with the first two types of investments – equity and debt.

STEP 2

Investing in equities

Equity

EQUITY IS AN ASSET CLASS THAT BROADLY RELATES TO INVESTING in stocks of companies.

But what exactly is a stock? Simply speaking, a stock is a share in the ownership of a company. When you own a stock, you effectively own a piece or share of the company – you have a claim on the company's assets and earnings.

Companies will often issue different classes of stock. The two basic kinds are ***common stock*** and ***preferred stock***. ***Common stock*** represents your ownership in a company, gives you a claim on dividends, and it also gives you one vote for each share you own to elect the board members.

Preferred stock also gives you ownership but does not represent voting rights.

In this chapter, we will limit our discussions to common stock.

As you acquire more stock in the company, your ownership stake goes up. This does not mean that you have a say in the day-to-day running of the business. So owning shares of Reliance does not mean that you can call Mukesh Ambani and tell him how to run the company, but you are entitled to one vote per share to elect a board of directors who can represent your thoughts and views at an annual meeting.

And, by the way, it doesn't really matter whether you say shares, equity or stock. They are all essentially the same thing.

- Every publicly listed company offers you, as a member of the public, the opportunity to own shares or equity. For the company, this is an opportunity to raise money using your investment. For you, it's an opportunity to invest your money in a company rather than a savings deposit, to enjoy the returns associated with this company as it grows.
- Some companies may not pay dividends; after all, they have no legal obligation to do so. In this situation, the only way you can make money on a stock is by holding on to it in the hope that it appreciates in the financial markets. On the other hand, the company might file for bankruptcy, in which case your shares are worth nothing.
- The value of a company's shares fluctuates with the markets, the economy and also other factors, like changes in the government and its policies. Public markets fluctuate with the state of the economy. Realistically, you must be aware

that the price of company shares can go down as much as they can go up, especially in the short term.

- Investing in equities is definitely more risky. However, with a calculated risk, you can expect higher returns. If you are willing to bear this risk for the long term, you are likely to reap a higher return. When an agent tells you that a particular stock will reap long-term benefits, they probably mean a time span well over two to four years, so please don't consider one year as long-term.

STEP 2A

Understanding company stock tables

YOU HAVE PROBABLY SEEN STOCK TABLES IN THE 'MONEY' section of your newspaper and chances are that most of the time you have skipped this section in favour of other, more interesting news. We are going to change that by demystifying the language of stock tables for you.

Stock tables are actually loaded with information that can help you become a savvy investor as long as you know how to interpret them. Each newspaper lists its financial tables a little differently, but they are all updated daily and give you clues about the current state of a particular company.

How to read a stock table

52W high	52W low	Stock	Ticker	Yield Div	%	P/E	Vol 00s	High	Low	Close	Net Chg
s45.39	19.75	ResMed	RMD			52.5	3831	42.00	39.51	41.50	–1.90
11.63	3.55	Revion A	REV				162	6.09	5.90	6.09	+0.12
77.25	55.13	RioTinto	RTP	2.30	3.2		168	72.75	71.84	72.74	+0.03
31.31	16.63	RitchleBr	RBA			20.9	15	24.49	24.29	24.49	–0.01
8.44	1.75	RiteAld	RAD				31028	4.50	4.20	4.31	+0.21
s38.63	18.81	RobtHalf	RHI			26.5	6517	27.15	26.50	26.50	+0.14
51.25	27.69	Rockwell	ROK	1.02	2.1	14.5	6412	47.99	47.00	47.54	+0.24

Here are the important things to look for when trying to learn about your stocks on a stock table.

Stock Name

Every stock is listed by its company name. Typically, this is abbreviated. See the column named 'Stock' in the table above.

Ticker

Each company has a unique alphabetic symbol called a ticker, which identifies the stock. It is important to know and recognize these tickers as you will refer to them when you buy and sell the stock. If you watch any business channel, you will see something called a ticker tape moving across the screen, quoting the latest prices for the stock alongside the ticker.

Dividend

A dividend, as you know, is the cash distribution in rupees that a company pays a shareholder for a share. The dividend per share listed on the stock table is the total dividend of the company divided by its average number of shares. See the column named 'Div' in the table on the previous page.

Volume

This shows you how many shares of that stock were traded that day. Volume is usually quoted in 100s.

Yield

Yield refers to the income return on an equity investment. Expressed as a percentage, it is calculated by dividing the annual dividend by the stock price. This is a unit that changes every day. Yield is always expressed as a percentage of the value of the stock and is always reported as if you are buying the stock that day. See the column named '%' in the table.

Closing Price

This tells you the price that the stock closed at on the day it was listed. See the column named 'Close' in the table.

Net Change

This tells you how the stock price ended today, compared with its price at the end of the last trading day.

52-week High/Low

The 52-week high gives you the highest price that the stock has reached in the most recent 52-week period. Conversely, the 52-week low gives you the lowest price that the stock has reached in the most recent 52-week period. So, together, these two units of information give you a range of price fluctuations of the stock over the last year. This is useful information, because when the price falls, it could be an indication that the company has problems, or it could signal a buying opportunity for the stock. See the first two columns of the table on p. 92.

P/E Ratio

This is the Price/Earnings ratio. Price refers to the price or the cost of a single share of the stock. Earnings refers to the company's earnings per share as reported in the most recent quarter.

The P/E ratio is an extremely important barometer in the world of stock investing as it tells you whether the stock is expensive or one of good value. The lower the ratio, the cheaper the stock. P/E depends upon the growth of the company.

It's worth taking a little time to understand the concept of P/E ratios because though you will find them in practically every stock table and quote, they can be tricky to interpret.

P/E Ratio = Market Value per Share/Earnings per Share

Most of the time, stock tables refer to something called a ***trailing P/E ratio***. This simply means that the P/E ratio has been calculated using earnings per share (EPS) from the last four quarters.

Even though the EPS is based upon past performance, the P/E ratio takes into account market expectations for a company's future growth. After all, one key truth about stock prices is that they reflect what investors think a company will be worth.

If a company has a P/E higher than the market or industry average, this means that the market is expecting big growth for this company over the next few months or years. A company with a high P/E ratio will eventually have to live up to the high rating by increasing its earnings or by dropping its stock price.

In India, the best performing IT companies tend to have

Microsoft and YAHOO!

Take Microsoft, for instance. Several years ago, when it was growing in leaps and bounds, its P/E ratio was over 100. Today, Microsoft is one of the largest companies in the world, so its revenues and earnings can't maintain the same growth as before. As a result, its P/E had dropped to 43 by June 2002. This reduction in the P/E ratio is a common occurrence as high-growth start-ups solidify their reputations and turn into blue chips.

Yahoo, on the other hand, was a stock very much in demand but as competition in the industry grew, Yahoo could not keep up – its P/E dropped and it became cheaper to buy as people began expecting less out of it.

higher P/E ratios as people are expecting more from them. It is the same with some of the newer private-sector banks. So the P/E ratios of Infosys or HDFC might be relatively high, but an infrastructure company like TISCO might have a lower P/E ratio, because investors do not have spectacular expectations. The same goes for shipping or mining companies.

According to Kenneth Andrade, Head – Investment, IDFC Asset Management, '*Take any mining stock – say at the end of a 10-year period you have mined away everything so the terminal value at Year 10 is ₹0. In Year 1, the earning potential will be maximum – say 10x. By Year 7, the earning potential will have dropped to, say, 3x because there is hardly anything left to mine. Naturally, the P/E will drop and the stock will become cheaper but that's because you are expecting less out of it.*'

Now, as we said before, the higher the P/E ratio, the more expensive it is to buy the stock. For example, a ₹10 stock with a P/E of 75 is much more 'expensive' than a ₹100 stock with a P/E of 20. That said, comparing two companies just by P/E ratio can be misleading.

It is nearly impossible to consider whether a company's P/E ratio is high or low without considering three main things about the company:

1. How fast has the company been growing in the past?
2. Are these rates expected to increase, or at least continue, in the future?
   (Something isn't right if a company has only grown at 5% in the past and yet has a very high P/E. In such a case, the stock might be overpriced).
3. Are you comparing two companies in the same industry?

It is only useful to compare companies if they are in the same industry. For example, utility companies are considered to be 'boring' by the investor community. They typically have low multiples because they are low-growth, stable industries. Contrast this to hi-tech industries that are characterized by phenomenal growth rates and constant change. Comparing a tech company to a utility company is a classic case of trying to compare apples to oranges. Given this, it is a good idea to compare high-growth companies to others in the same industry, or to the industry average.

Meanwhile, saying that a high P/E ratio means a stock is overvalued or a low P/E ratio means the stock is undervalued is far too simplistic. A low P/E ratio could also mean that the market believes the company is headed for trouble in the near future. After all, when stocks go down, they usually do so for a reason. It could be that a company has warned that earnings will come in lower than expected.

WHAT THE EXPERTS SAY

'If the price of a stock is ₹100 and your earnings are ₹10 per share then your P/E ratio is 10 (100/10 = 10). This means, assuming that the company doesn't grow at all, you will get returns at 10%. Now take a bond – at the end of 10 years, you get your principal and a fixed 10% return for 10 years. It might seem that you can make a 10% return having invested in either bonds or equities. In reality, the company should grow, so your equity investment will have the probability of earning more. Of course, this could go up and down a little each year.

You have to think about the price you are going to pay for the underlying earning. If you think it's going to be higher, pay a higher amount for it (that is buy a stock with a higher P/E); if you think it'll go lower, pay a lower price for it (that is buy a stock with a lower P/E). There is no fixed rule saying that a lower P/E is better than a higher one – in the same industry, one company might be able to grow faster than the other. Don't make the mistake of comparing two companies in different sectors because their dynamics are different.'

– **Kenneth Andrade**

Head – Investment, IDFC Asset Management

Again, it all comes down to research. You have to know the company you're investing in inside out to figure out why the P/E is high or low at any given point of time. Where in its growth cycle is this company? How much growth can you expect from the industry? Is the stock cheap because the company is in a relatively early growth stage, or is it a danger sign that earnings will be low because of other economic shocks? If the ratio is high, is the stock overvalued or is this a company that could help change the face of the world as we know it?

Ask yourself these questions over and over again, and coordinate your research to arrive at a considered decision.

P/E is a useful tool to analyse a company but interpreting it correctly is critical as well.

How to read a stock quote

You can understand a lot about the performance of a stock by looking directly at its daily stock quote. It is a good idea to get into the habit of doing this with stocks that you own.

There are several financial websites where you can look up stock quotes – Reuters, Google Finance and Bloomberg – or you can look them up directly on the stock exchange website.

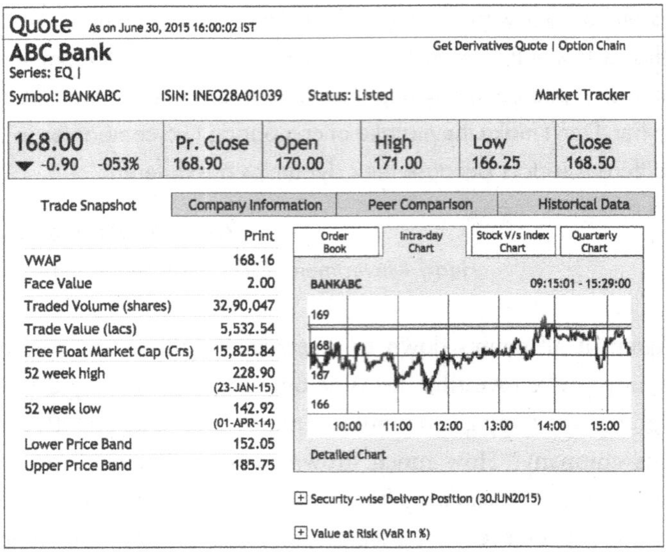

Consider this example from the NSE website:

Here are the items that are listed

Current Price

The current price of the stock is listed in the largest font. In this example, it is ₹168. It also shows that the closing price was down by 53%.

Previous Close

This is the previous day's closing price – ₹168.90

Open

This shows what the stock opened at on this day – ₹170

High

This shows the highest price reached during the day – ₹171

Low

This shows the lowest price the stock reached that day – ₹166.25

Close

This shows the price the stock closed at that day – ₹168.50

Trade Snapshot

The trade snapshot appears on the left-hand side and shows some details that are similar to what we find in the stock tables, such as the 52-week high and low, and the upper and lower price bands.

Charts

The right-hand side shows three charts: The 'intra-day chart' shows how the stock has moved up and down over the course of the day. The 'stock versus index chart' shows the performance of the stock in comparison to the Nifty, which is the flagship index of the National Stock Exchange. The 'quarterly chart' shows the performance of the stock over the last quarter.

Bulls and Bears

It's good to get to acquainted with these two terms as they will form an unavoidable part of your stock market vocabulary.

A ***bull market*** refers to a period when the economy is booming. Investors are confident and 'charge forward at high speed like an excited bull' to buy stocks because they expect them to rise in price.

A ***bear market***, on the other hand, refers to a declining market when the economy slows down due to recession or low employment levels. Investors become pessimistic and approach the markets with the 'slow and lumbering movements of a bear'.

Of course, the daily upswings and downswings of the market are not to be confused for bull and bear reactions of the market.

KEY POINTS TO REMEMBER

- Choose your mode of trading. It can be online, through your computer and an internet connection, or offline, through a phone and a broker.
- If you plan to trade online, make sure you have a demat account, and both your demat account and your bank account are connected to your trading account.

- Be prepared to spend time and effort researching the companies and industries whose stocks you want to invest in.
- Be fully aware of short- and long-term capital gains as well as risks when it comes to investing in stocks.
- If you plan to invest in the primary market through an IPO (IPO stands for initial public offering and refers to the launch of a company's shares on the stock market), make sure the IPO is really worthy of your investment. Ensure that your research is thorough.
- If you plan to invest in the secondary market by buying shares of a company that is listed on a stock exchange, research the future prospects of the company.
- Having a working knowledge of analytical tools allows you to have a more measured and logical approach towards investing. It also allows you to track the performance of your investments on your own, which, in turn, helps you get over the fear of investing.
- Tools like P/E are only indicative in nature and can be interpreted in a number of ways.

STEP 2B

Understanding stock exchanges and indices

A STOCK EXCHANGE IS A HIGHLY ORGANIZED ELECTRONIC marketplace, where stockbrokers and traders can buy and sell stocks, bonds and other securities. There are a number of stock exchanges in India but the two most significant are the ***Bombay Stock Exchange (BSE)*** and the ***National Stock Exchange (NSE)***. Both the BSE and the NSE offer opportunities for trading financial products, either individual equities or any cluster of stocks gathered into their wide offering of index products. Financial indices are constructed to measure the price movements of stocks, bonds and other kinds of investments.

A stock market index is an index comprising a cluster of stocks that represents the whole market, or one specific segment of the market. These indices are meant to capture the overall behaviour of equity markets. The index is essentially a mode of monitoring whether stock values have gone up or down. It is calculated with reference to a base period and a base index value. The BSE's flagship index is the ***Sensex*** (derived from 'sensitive index') and NSE's flagship index is the ***Nifty***.

The BSE and the Sensex

The BSE is located on Dalal Street in Mumbai. Established in 1875, it is the tenth largest stock market in the world as of January 2015.

The BSE has many different types of indices which are essentially indicators that show you whether the value of a cluster of stocks has gone up or down. The Sensex, its flagship index, shows you the performance of the major companies listed on the BSE.

The Sensex – also known as the ***S&P BSE Sensex*** or the ***BSE 30*** – is a market index of 30 well-established and financially sound companies listed on the BSE. These 30 companies comprise some of the largest and most actively traded stocks in India, representing a variety of industrial sectors. This index is traded not just on the BSE but also in financial markets abroad.

If the value of the Sensex rises, it means that the prices of stocks of most of the major companies on the BSE have gone up. If the value of the Sensex goes down, it means that the prices of stocks of most of the major companies on the BSE have gone down.

Many lay investors will invest in one or more of the company stocks that make up the Sensex. As such, this is a good starting point for furthering your understanding of the equity markets.

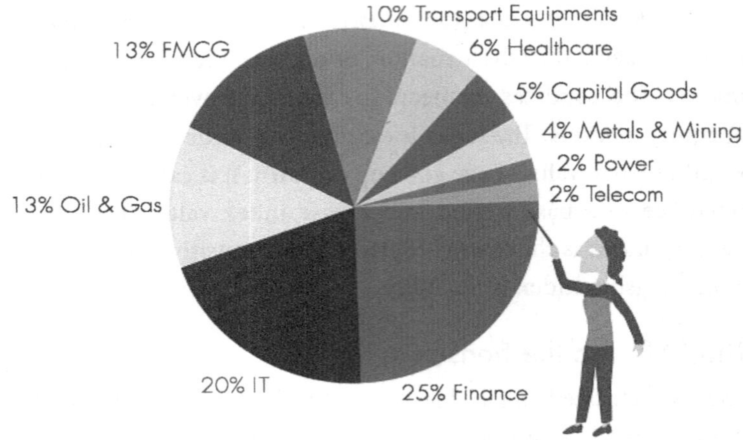

Sector-wise distribution of Sensex stocks

The Sensex: A Volatile Journey

It is incredibly important to understand that financial markets are volatile, meaning that they will fluctuate with the state of the economy. Obviously then, the Sensex, which is an index of stocks that tracks the performance of India's public financial markets, is going to be volatile, too.

What does this mean for an investor? Let's look at Suneela's case.

Suneela was keen to invest her money in equities and did so in October 1999. At the time, the Sensex was riding high at around 5,000 points. However, the very next year, when the media uncovered the Ketan Parekh scam, the Sensex immediately dropped about 60% or so to 2,000 points. Suneela was devastated. Her reason for investing in equities was to get a higher return but exactly the opposite had happened, and all within the course of a year. Scarred by the incident, she was tempted to pull out her equity investment. '*Never again did I want to touch equities,*' she says. '*I didn't have all the money in the world to gamble with and wanted to put it into safe investments.*'

A friend of Suneela's convinced her not to pull out her money. There was no point, she was told, the markets were already so low that she might as well wait it out to see what would happen. Suneela was reluctant at first but she did wait it out, and by 2004 the Sensex had risen once again to 6,000 points. So, even though Suneela had not made any money from her initial investment, she was happy that she hadn't lost it all.

By 2006, the Sensex had reached 10,000 and in January 2008, it hit an all-time high of above 21,000. Suneela was over the moon. Her investment was up by 25–30%.

Seeing Suneela's gains, her friend Neelam was in complete awe and decided to put some of her money in equities as well, to reap the same benefits as Suneela. Other friends pulled their money out of equity investments at the time, since they had reached their financial goals but Suneela decided not to follow the herd. '*My investments were doing so well, I thought why pull them out now. Some people were talking about a recession in the US but I thought, how is that going to affect me here?*' she recalls.

Unfortunately, it did. Significantly, that was the year the Sensex went into free fall. Suneela was shattered when the Sensex plunged to 8,000 points by the last quarter of the year. '*I was back to square one. My earnings were lost and I thought my investment was gone for good,*' she says. Well, that was probably a good thing. The fact that she considered her earnings lost for good meant that she had no incentive to pull out her money from the stock markets, unlike her friend, Neelam, who was so alarmed by the situation that she took out all her money immediately and invested it in fixed income products.

In April 2014, the Sensex finally crossed 22,000 points, and following the BJP's landslide victory in the national elections, it reached record highs of 25,000 – Suneela had completely ridden the wave.

So what's the key point you've learnt from Suneela's example?

If you are going to invest in equities, stay long-term, at least 3 to 5 years, according to Kenneth Andrade, because that's how much time it takes to ride out an equities-market cycle. Of course, the longer you stay invested, the lower your chances of loss and the more you stand to gain, given that equities work on the principle of compounding.

Andrade insists that it is wrong to move your money into debt out of fear because the behaviour of equity markets invariably affects other asset classes, too.

To clarify, he explains, '*If markets fall and you feel your money is not safe in equities, it is definitely not going to be safe in bank deposits either, because the companies you have invested in are not going to be able to repay the debt on their balance sheets to the bank lenders when their stock prices are low. So how can your bank deposits be good? The markets always come back and equities have to come back first. In retrospect, Suneela made more in equities than Neelam who moved her investment to debt when the Sensex fell to 8,000, because the equity markets came back first.*'

'*It's important to remember that when you buy equities you aren't simply investing in a stock price. You are buying a participating share of the profit of a company which is represented by that stock price. Effectively, you are buying a business. When you buy a number of stocks, remember one thing – they are not all going to collapse and stay collapsed. The key thing is to give it time and understand how the behaviour of equities impacts other asset classes. It's not about buying stock or companies; it's about buying into an entire financial ecosystem,'* he adds.

WHAT THE EXPERTS SAY

'Investing in equities is all about participation. Your objective is to either participate with the markets or beat them. So, if you put 70% of your investment rupees into index products like the Sensex then you are participating in a more passive sense. If you invest in mutual funds, note how your investment manager will always talk to you about trying to participate with the index or to actively beat it. I would say you should put 70% of your investment in an index fund where you can participate, and with the balance try to actively do better than the index.'

– **Kenneth Andrade**
Head – Investment, IDFC Asset Management

The NSE

The National Stock Exchange was set up in Mumbai in the 1990s to serve as a fully electronic stock exchange. Just as the Sensex is the BSE's flagship index, the NSE also has a flagship index known as the ***S&P CNX Nifty*** or ***Nifty 50*** or just the ***Nifty***, offering investors in India and around the world the opportunity to gain exposure to the Indian financial markets.

The Nifty represents 50 different companies in 22 industry sectors. As a single financial product, it includes a variety of investment sub-categories – exchange traded funds, futures, and options and derivatives. The Nifty is owned and operated by India

Index Services & Products Limited (IISL), which is a joint venture between the NSE and Credit Rating Information Services of India Limited (CRISIL).

FAQs about stock exchange and indices

There are other stock exchanges in the country, such as the Calcutta Stock Exchange. However, these are not as popular as the BSE and the NSE.

There are also other indices for mid-cap stocks, such as the BSE mid-cap index for metal stocks and fast-moving consumer goods (FMCG) stocks.

Q What is the criteria used by the Sensex and the Nifty to include companies on their listing?

Both the Sensex and the Nifty use strict criteria when selecting a stock to include in their indices. They take into account things like:

- How long the company has been public (determined by when it first listed its stock).
- How frequently the stock is traded – typically, with these flagship indices, trading happens on a daily, even hourly basis.
- The company's rank based on the market capitalization of companies (that is, the total value of shares issued by the company, determined by multiplying the number of shares by the value of each share). A company should be in the top 100 to feature on these indices.
- The industry sector to which the company shares belong – both flagship indices try to have a diversified portfolio of industry segments.
- The historical record of the company and its shares.

Q How do stock exchanges benefit the community?

Stock exchanges benefit the community in a number of different ways.

According to Subhankar Nandan of the Loyola Academy of Investment Management, '*They aid economic development by providing a ready pool of interested investors; they aid companies by attracting funds and enhancing their reputation via public listing; they enable the government to create capital for projects of national importance by selling securities on the exchanges; and they enable central banks to control credit by buying and selling securities on the stock exchanges.*'

And this is how stock exchanges benefit you as the investor:

- Equities are highly liquid investments. Stock exchanges allow you to stay liquid.
- Securities traded on stock exchanges are often good collateral for loans. This can come in handy if you need to apply for a home loan or an education loan.
- The strict rules and regulations of the stock exchanges safeguard the interests of investors. This is why investing in flagship indices like the Nifty and the Sensex are beneficial for both beginners and seasoned investors.
- You can easily calculate the net worth of your investments by looking at daily stock quotations.
- While investing in equities is risky, you help mitigate that risk by purchasing listed securities.[1]

Q Why do stock prices change?

Basically, there is no consensus as to why stock prices change but we know that they do so every single day as a result of market forces. Essentially, this has to do with the economic laws of supply and demand – if more people want to buy a stock, the price will naturally move up. But if more people want to sell a stock than buy it, then supply will exceed demand and the price will fall.

Pretty simple, huh? But then there are other factors that influence stock prices. These are:

Tastes and Preferences

More people might want to buy a certain stock because they like the company better than other companies. Why? Is this on a whim, or because they think it represents a sector that will do really well?

Let's take the example of Reliance. Many people bought Reliance stock because they believed that the company was providing essential services for the betterment of the economy.

Sometimes decisions can be quite personal. Many people put their money into Starbucks several years ago. At the time, the reason was two-fold: they liked coffee, and figured that others around the world would also like the Starbucks mode of functioning as it promoted a lifestyle which appealed to people. That was over 10 years ago, and the Starbucks stock has gone up multiple times since then.

Contingencies

Real-estate bubbles, tech bubbles, scandals like the Harshad Mehta or Ketan Parekh scam in late 1999–2000 and, of course, elections affect stock prices. Stock prices are bound to rise with a happy outcome of parliamentary elections and fall during the reverse. Following the swearing in of the Narendra Modi-led BJP government, the Sensex crossed the 25,000 mark for the first time. Essentially, the price movement of a stock indicates what investors feel the company is worth. A lot of this is based on emotional factors – fear, greed or a pure 'feel-good' sentiment.

Rumours

Sometimes bad news is released about a company, which affects other companies as well. For example, the Satyam scandal relating to falsification of records, conspiracy, cheating and insider trading drove the company's stock down by 78% in a single day in January 2009. It also affected other stocks, especially those in the IT sector, and the Sensex was driven down 7%.

Performance

Remember, however, that the most important thing affecting the value of a company is the profit it makes, or its earnings. Public companies are required to report their earnings four times a year during what is known in investment analysis terms as 'earnings season'. Investment analysts await earnings each season, because if a company's earnings are better than expected, the stock price is likely to rise, whereas if a company's results disappoint the stock price falls.

So, the bottom line is that nobody knows for sure why stock prices change. Some remain steadfast, in that there is no financial jyotishi or astrologer out there who can predict how stock prices will change. Others make a living out of generating charts based on past price movements which they believe will predict future trends, determining when to buy and sell. As a lay investor, it is best to avoid the latter.

Your Money Mantra

An index can be a good focal point for monitoring your investments as well as giving you a general idea of where the market is headed. Reading these signs will enable you to have a proper investment plan.

- Equities are volatile assets and anything that promises you high returns also carries high risk. It's all about how you manage them.
- There is no way you can avoid the volatility factor when you invest in stocks, but you can always plan in order to minimize your risk.
- Various factors like economics, emotions or rumours might seem unrelated at first, but these can affect your investments. Monitor the index to see how other securities are doing before making your decision.
- Even if the market tanks, the equities are the first to bounce back as the companies have to make a profit in order to pay their debts so carefully consider your steps ahead even when the situation seems dire.

STEP 2C

Your equity investment checklist

✓ Choose the right company

Investing wisely is all about research. Carry out research on a large pool of companies. Study their public financial statements, look at profit and loss forecasts by analysts and experts. Think about how things like technology, social change, inflation or rupee fluctuations and market sentiment might affect them. Once you have done this research thoroughly, choose two or three such companies from this pool to invest in each year.

✓ Don't follow the herd

As tempting as it is to do what your friends do, it's not a good idea to always follow the herd. All of us have different priorities and investment appetites, not to mention varying capacities to invest in the first place. Chart out your own unique path based upon your goals and risk-profile, because it's your goals and risk-profile that truly define your specific needs as an investor.

✓ Be an investor not a speculator

A speculator is someone who puts money into the market for the short-term, hoping to make a quick return in a hurry, betting on the fact that market fluctuations will work to her advantage. An investor, on the other hand, goes into the market for the long-term. She isn't worried about daily fluctuations and will hold on to her stocks for a lengthy period of time until they reach her predetermined target price. Speculation forces you to take risks whereas investment teaches you to manage risks.

✓ Grab opportunities

Volatility is the essence of equity markets. When markets go down it is easy to get depressed but, in truth, this is your opportunity for purchasing stocks at a low price. Keep a small window of your investment portfolio open for such opportunities. Be careful, however, that you do this only with a small portion of your investment fund and not your entire kitty.

✓ History does not predict the future

'History repeats itself' is a well-known adage but it does not work this way in financial markets. There is no point trying to analyse past stock market performances to predict which way the markets will move in the future. Different times bring forth different economic situations. The only thing we can learn from history is to watch out, perhaps, for scams. There is no crystal ball here that can predict the future.

✓ Monitor and review

Once you have invested in a stock, don't just let it sit there. Keep an eye on its performance. Keep tabs on the company you have bought into by reading its quarterly announcements. Review the reasons you bought this stock in the first place - have your objectives changed? Analyse your mistakes. You will make some along the way but let each one be an opportunity to help you emerge wiser the next time around.

STEP 3

Investing in debt securities

NALINI KURIAN HAD RETIRED FROM ITC IN THE EARLY 2000s, after 40 years of service. Over the course of her career, she had invested her money in a combination of bank fixed deposits and equities. The equity investments had really worked to her advantage, offering returns as high as 15% in some years.

But Nalini had ridden the waves and troughs of the stock market and knew too well that without a regular pay cheque she couldn't afford any risks. It was time for her to be more conservative. She was keen to invest her savings in a safe asset that would give her regular income.

A close friend advised her to go for a bank FD which offered an attractive 8% return – ideal, perhaps, at first glance.

Kartik Mohan, Nalini's investment advisor, didn't like the idea.

He suggested that tax-free bonds were the way to go. Issued by government or quasi-government agencies, they were equally safe, and with a long-term tenure of 10, 15 or 20 years she'd earn a tax-free interest of 8.5 to 9.0% every year. Even though, on the face of it, an FD looked attractive enough with an 8% return, in reality, the net return after tax deductions would amount to about 5%, significantly less than what she would get with a bond.

Nalini's investment was phenomenally successful. With ₹50 lakh invested in bonds, she started getting a regular income of ₹4.5 lakh per year. Nalini didn't have a very lavish lifestyle, so her income from bonds was more than enough to meet her basic needs.

Inspired by her aunt's success with bonds, Nalini's 40-year-old niece, Janaki, wanted to follow suit so that she, too, could build a successful retirement corpus 20 years down the road. So Nalini introduced her to Kartik, who had helped her with her investment portfolio. Much to her surprise, he gave her a thumbs down, saying, '*What works for a retired person won't work for a woman in her younger years who is targeting a corpus 15 or 20 years down the line. In your 30s and 40s, you tend to spend any amount of annual income you get. So I'm hesitant to recommend it for younger women who want to actually grow their wealth.*'

Kartik insisted that a portfolio of primarily equity investments remained the best option for Janaki. '*Once she retires 10 to 15 years from now, we can review it. Until then, this is the best way for her to multiply her money,*' he said.

Types of debt securities

When it comes to debt securities, there is a range of options you can choose from. We've already discussed basic debt instruments like bank and company FDs. Added to this are other types of debt, like company loans or leases and public sector or government debt instruments.

A ***lease*** is an arrangement in which the owner of the asset transfers the rights of use of the asset to the debtor for a certain period of time in exchange for regular payment. Many people lease an apartment, or a computer, or even a car.

Debentures are unsecured debt securities issued by companies in return for monetary interest, and ***bonds*** are fixed-income instruments that offer a regular rate of interest in addition to guaranteeing the return of your principal amount at the end of the bond tenure.

Worldwide, debt markets are three to four times larger than equity markets. However, the debt market in India is very small in comparison to the equity market. This is because the domestic debt market was liberalized just recently and is still in its nascent stage of development.

WHAT THE EXPERTS SAY

'Most investors, including women, prefer to invest their money in debt instruments such as bank deposits and government schemes, such as NSC and POS, which are considered safe. However, investors often don't realize that these instruments offer lower returns and, therefore, they need to consider instruments offering market-linked returns such as equity and bonds in order to beat inflation.'

– **Suresh Soni**

CEO, Deutsche Asset Management India Pvt. Ltd

The debt market in India

The debt market in India comprises two main segments: ***government securities*** and ***corporate securities***.

Government Securities

Government securities dominate the Indian debt market with government borrowings amounting to a 70% share. The government needs to raise funds for macroeconomic projects, so it will often issue bonds of different interest rates and tenures. Individual investors like you and I cannot invest directly in government bonds. Instead, we must purchase these through banks, provident funds and insurance companies like the LIC.

- Major participants in a government securities market include banks, insurance companies, mutual funds, financial institutions, Indian corporates, foreign institutional investors (FIIs), PFs and the RBI.
- There are two types of central government securities in India – ***short-term treasury bills*** and ***long-term government bonds***. Since they come with a sovereign guarantee, these are considered to have zero default risk. They are less volatile and generally offer higher returns than what you might get in a bank deposit.

Corporate Securities

India's corporate bond market is still dominated by private placements, which constitute 95% of the issuances. This is largely because of the ease, efficiency and significantly lower cost involved in comparison to public issuances. Public issuances gathered steam from 2009 and grew 11 times in the next four years, primarily due to tax incentives on infrastructure bonds (tax-free bonds and tax rebate under Section 88 of the Income Tax Act).

Retail participation in government securities - including tax-free bonds and bonds which offer tax rebates - is on the rise. However, its share of direct retail participation is still not significant when compared to the overall market. Secondary market trading in retail bonds is yet to catch up. Apart from bonds, investors can also choose from a variety of other debt securities, which offer a range of products with liquidity, such as mutual funds.

In the following chapter, we will examine investing in bonds in detail.

STEP 3A

Investing in bonds

BONDS ARE PERHAPS THE MOST INTERESTING DEBT INSTRUMENTS to invest in.

When you purchase a bond, you are essentially loaning money to the issuer of the bond, say a company or the government. The price of the bond is the amount of money being loaned when it is first issued and is known as the bond's ***face value***. In return for that loan, the issuer pays you a periodic interest or coupon. Bonds are issued for a specific period of time – a year, three years, ten years or more. At the end of this time period, the bond matures, and the issuer repays you the full amount of your principal.

Bonds are particularly popular because, unlike equities, which rely upon the volatility of stock markets, bonds are considered to be 'safe'. But that's not to say there is no risk involved in investing in bonds. In fact, the higher the coupon rate on a bond, the more risk it is likely to carry.

'Debt securities are generally considered to have low levels of risk as compared to equity securities,' says Suresh Soni, CEO, Deutsche Asset Management India Pvt. Ltd. *'Again, in debt securities, there are various instruments with varying levels of risk but there is always an element of risk no matter how negligible it may be. For example, liquid funds are considered to have a negligible level of risk.'*

Bonds and the prevailing interest rate

The interest rates on any kind of debt security can change with different market conditions. A bond's price is also subject to these fluctuations. But why do bond prices fluctuate?

More than anything else, bond prices depend on the prevailing interest rate in the economy set by the RBI. If interest rates rise, the prices of bonds in the market fall. So the value of coupons of bonds that have already been issued will rise to bring them in line with the newer bonds that have just been issued with higher-value coupons. Again, if interest rates fall, bond prices in the market rise; so that the yield of the older bonds that have been issued earlier drops to bring them in line with newer bonds just issued with lower-value coupons.

Another thing you must remember is that the longer a bond's period to maturity, the more its prices can fluctuate with the markets. If you decide to buy or sell a bond, its traded price will differ from its face value.

A bond's interest rate or coupon rate shows the return you get on a bond. When you buy a bond at face value, the coupon is equal to the interest rate but if the bond price changes then so does the yield.

So if you buy a bond with a 10% coupon at its ₹1,000 par value, the yield is 10% (₹100 for ₹1,000). Pretty simple, so far. But if the price goes down to ₹800, then the coupon goes up to 12.5%. This happens so that you can still get that guaranteed ₹100 return on an asset that is now worth ₹800. On the other hand, if the bond goes up in price to ₹1,200, the coupon shrinks to 8.33% to give you a return of ₹100 on ₹1,200.

High coupons and high prices both sound pretty good, so you are probably wondering how this works, given that they cannot both happen at the same time. Well, that depends entirely on your point of view. If you are a bond buyer and you pay ₹800 for a bond worth ₹1,000, and end up with a high yield of 12.5%, you have successfully been able to buy your bond at a cheaper price. But if you already own a bond and you've locked in your interest rate, you'll have to keep your fingers crossed that the price of the bond goes up. Why? Because this allows you to cash in by selling your bond in the future at a higher price than what you originally paid for it.

If you invest in bonds with the idea of holding them until maturity, this may not affect you as much because you are guaranteed your principal. That said, when you invest in bonds, you are typically given a ***yield to maturity***, which is a more advanced yield calculation showing the total return you can get if you hold on to the bond till it matures. This is equal to all the interest payments you will receive plus any gain if you purchased the bond at a discount, or loss if you purchased it at a higher price. It's the one thing you need to examine carefully in order to accurately compare different bonds with different maturities and coupons.

What are the various types of bonds you can invest in?

Bonds can be issued by Public Sector Units (PSUs), the government or companies that are looking to raise capital. ***Government bonds*** are issued and backed by the Government of India. They are also known as G-Sec. Typically, they pay a return of 7% to 10%. Their maturity period can be anywhere between three months to 30 years.

Bonds issued by PSUs are called ***PSU bonds***. They are medium- to long-term bonds (which carry a fixed or a floating rate of interest), or sometimes deep discount bonds. Typically, they are issued only through private placements or to institutional investors, so your portfolio might have some indirect exposure to PSUs if, in fact, you have invested in a mutual fund, a PF, or an insurance company that has invested in a PSU. Once it has been issued, however, you can buy and sell it in the secondary market.

Regular income bonds

These bonds provide a stable source of income at regular, pre-determined intervals. They also include corporate bonds, which are considered less safe than government bonds as the issuing companies are subject to market and industry ups and downs (just as they are when you purchase stocks). Companies can also issue convertible bonds that can be converted into a pre-defined number of stock or just regular, non-convertible bonds.

These brands can be taxable or tax-free. You can choose the bond depending upon your tax status.

Also, you may come across something called ***deep discount bonds***. These bonds don't make regular payments to investors but accumulate the earnings and pay a pre-defined sum after a few years.

Tax-saving Bonds

These bonds are considered to be low-risk with an interest rate of around 8%. Also, they can be included in your tax deduction. This means that the initial investment in such bonds is exempt from tax, and can be reduced from taxable income. However, the interest component is still taxable. These include tax-saving infrastructure bonds which are issued by non-banking finance corporations (NBFCs) to procure funds to invest in government infrastructure projects.

Infrastructure bonds are long-term investment bonds that work in the same way as FDs, but instead of a bank you end up investing your money with an NBFC for the tenure of the bond. With a maturity period of 10 or 15 years, they are reasonably safe and offered by leading financial institutions or large infrastructure companies and can be bought and sold through your demat account.

Tax-free Bonds

Another type of bond is a tax-free bond where the deduction on the initial investment is not available but the interest income is tax free.[4] These are mostly issued by government enterprises and they pay a fixed coupon or interest rate. As the bond proceeds are invested in infrastructure projects, they typically have a long-term maturity period of 10, 15 or even 20 years. The interest on these bonds is paid annually and their credit risk is considered to be quite low since they are mostly issued by government-backed companies.

It is important to note that these bonds are not completely tax-free; only the interest earned on them is tax-free. Any capital gain from a short-term sale in the secondary market is still liable for tax. PSUs regularly issue tax-free bonds. Some PSUs that frequently issue tax-free bonds include Indian Railway Finance Corporation (IRFC), Power Finance Corporation (PFC) and Housing & Urban Development Corporation (HUDCO). For a current list of bonds including tax-free bonds, you should visit the National Stock Exchange website.

Why you should invest in government debt

Although corporate bonds are available in abundance, if you are looking at investing in debt securities, you should definitely consider government debt securities.

The biggest reason for investing in government securities is the 'zero default risk', also known as ***Gilt-Edged Securities*** or ***Gilts***. Government securities do not attract deduction of TDS and you needn't file a return only to obtain a TDS refund. Their maturity period can range from a few months up to 30 years and this sort of long-term investment provides more opportunities for diversification.

Bond credit rating system

Bonds have an alphanumeric credit rating system which ranks them as either investment grade or below investment grade. While this system is not one hundred per cent foolproof it does give you a fair idea of the risk factor associated with the bond and the credit-worthiness of the company issuing it. Investment grade bonds are obviously much less risky than non-investment grade bonds, but as with all investment options, with low risk comes a lower return.

Credit ratings are issued by credit rating agencies such as Fitch Ratings Inc., CARE (Credit Analysis and Research Ltd), ICRA

Limited or CRISIL, and are indicative of the rating agency's opinion on the likelihood of the bond being paid back completely on the maturity date. The ***Securities and Exchange Board of India*** (SEBI) mandates all companies that issue corporate bonds and debentures to the public to get themselves rated. What's more, once the company issuances cross ₹100 crore they typically need to get two ratings from two different rating companies.

Ratings companies consider various types of risks pertaining to the particular industry sector a company belongs to, the specific business it is in and other financial risks pertaining to its profit, loss and cash flow. CRISIL, for example, assigns credit ratings to debt obligations on three basic scales: the long-term scale, the short-term scale and the fixed deposit scale. CRISIL's long-term credit rating scale and the description associated with each category on the rating scale is given below.

Symbol (Rating category)	**Description (Likelihood of meeting debt obligations on time)**
AAA	Highest Safety
AA	High Safety
A	Adequate Safety
BBB	Moderate Safety
BB	Inadequate Safety
B	High Risk
C	Substantial Risk
D	Default

FAQs about credit ratings[5]

Q *Is credit rating a recommendation to invest in a debt instrument?*

A credit rating is not a recommendation to buy, hold, or sell a debt instrument. It's simply one tool you can employ to make an investment decision.

Q *What is the difference between credit rating and equity research?*
Credit ratings are assigned to debt instruments, while equity research relates to shares. A credit rating focuses on the risk of non-payment, the primary variable in debt instruments. Equity research focuses on growth possibilities as that is what drives equity evaluations.

Q *Does a credit rating assure repayment?*
A credit rating is not an assurance of repayment of the rated instrument. Rather, it is an opinion on the relative degree of risk associated with such repayment. This opinion represents a probable estimate of the likelihood of default.

Q *Who regulates a rating agency?*
The capital market regulator regulates rating agencies in most regions. In India, the capital markets regulator SEBI regulates the rating agencies in the country.

Q *How do investors benefit from a credit rating?*
Credit ratings help investors facilitate comparative assessment of the available investment options and allow them to monitor the assets.

How to read a bond table

As with stock tables, different newspapers and print media format their bond tables a little differently but all of them have the same basic information. On the following page you will see what a bond table looks like at Reuters.

ISIN	SECURITY	COUPON	MATURITY DATE	LAST TRD PRICE	WTD AVG YIELD	CUM. VOL IN MLNS
BSE						
===						
INE514E08BC3	EXPORT-IMPORT BANK OF INDIA	9.32%	06-Jul-15	100.0063	8.3300	4.00
INE001A07NF9	HOUSING DEVELOPMENT FINANCE CORP	9.32%	10-Sep-15	100.1143	8.4200	750.00
INE118D07112	LAFARGE INDIA PVT. LTD	9.15%	12-Feb-16	100.2046	8.5300	260.00
INE020B07IX0	RURAL ELECTRI-FICATION CORPORATION	9.27%	08-Aug-16	100.8795	8.3700	500.00
INE134E08HL8	POWER FINANCE CORPORATION LTD	8.35%	27-May-17	99.9905	8.3400	200.00
INE752E07IC6	POWER GRID CORP. LTD	9.64%	31-May-17	102.7307	8.0400	100.00
INE514E08DA3	EXPORT-IMPORT BANK OF INDIA	9.28%	15-Oct-18	102.4018	8.3900	50.00
INE752E07ML9	POWER GRID CORPORATION OF INDIA	8.40%	27-May-19	99.5662	8.5300	200.00
NSE						
===						
INE001A07MQ8	HOUSING DEVELOP-MENT FINANCE CORP	8.95%	13-Jul-15	99.9995	8.2000	500.00
INE804I07FG3	ECL FINANCE LIMITED	NIFTY	20-Jul-15	169.4400	0.0000	2.80
INE895D08527	TATA SONS LIMITED	9.67%	31-Aug-15	100.1537	8.1450	50.00
INE001A07NF9	HOUSING DEVELOP-MENT FINANCE CORP	9.32%	10-Sep-15	100.1143	8.1499	1750.00
INE756I07225	HDB FINANCIAL SERVICES LIMITED	9.55%	25-Sep-15	100.3426	8.1565	800.00

BSE or NSE Code

This is a code identifying the bond security on the stock exchange on which it trades. That's what the first column in the table above gives you.

Issuer

This is the company that issues the bond shown as 'Security' in the table.

Coupon

The coupon is the fixed interest rate that the issuer of the bond pays to the lender.

Maturity Date

This is the date on which the issuer will repay the investors their principal.

Last Trade Price

This is the current price of the bond. This price is quoted in relation to 100, regardless of its face value. Think of the price as a percentage: A bond with a price of 93 is trading at 93% of its face value.

Weighted Average Yield

The weighted average yield shows the annual return until the bond matures. This is typically the yield to maturity and not the current yield.

WHAT THE EXPERTS SAY

'There are four measures that the lay female investor must consider when investing in bonds or debt instruments.

1. Maturity: Refers to the period of time the bond will take to pay the principal and accrued interest.
2. Yield: The rate of interest that will be paid on the bond and the frequency of interest payment, whether it is quarterly, half-yearly or annual.
3. Credit Rating: A credit rating indicates the likelihood of the bond issuer to repay on maturity. Higher-quality investment grade bonds tend to pay slightly lower interest rates, than lower-rated bonds, but also tend to have a much lower default rate.
4. Liquidity: Liquidity of the bond refers to how frequently the bond is traded in the market.'

– **Suresh Soni**

CEO, Deutsche Asset Management India Pvt. Ltd

Your Money Mantra

Debt securities, especially bonds, are a great alternative to build your portfolio. However, you should select them only if they suit your needs as an investor.

- Do not be taken in by the low-risk logic. Even though it might be negligible, the risk factor is still there.
- Though a great option in many ways, they pose the problem of liquidity and are not suitable for you if you are looking for easily available funding in the future.
- If you do not want to access debt securities directly, you can access them in the form of other hybrid investments such as mutual funds.

ARE BONDS A BETTER BET THAN STOCKS?

Buying bonds is an entirely different scenario from buying stocks, as you don't actually get to own a piece of the company. However, since, like a shareholder, you are also loaning to the company, you have a priority claim on assets like land or cash balances in case the company goes bankrupt.

So why bother with equity then, when bond deals look so much better? For the simple reason that, in the long term, you are likely to make more as an equity stakeholder than you are as a holder of bonds. But there are a number of reasons why it's a good idea to invest some of your portfolio in bonds.

- First of all, bonds help to preserve capital. Unless the company or the government that issues the bond goes bankrupt, it is highly likely that you'll receive the amount you originally invested.
- Secondly, bonds pay interest at fixed time intervals. This can be a valuable source of income if you are older, retired or do not have a monthly pay cheque coming in. For instance, if you buy ₹10 lakh worth of bonds that paid 8% interest annually (that would be ₹80,000 yearly), a fraction of that interest could be used either monthly or quarterly for your expenses.
- Bonds can also have a large tax advantage. When the government or a Public Sector Unit (PSU) issues various types of bonds to raise money to build bridges, roads, etc., the interest that is earned is usually tax-exempt.

But there is a catch. As Suresh Soni tells us, '*Buying bonds leaves you with liquidity issues. While bonds may be listed, they are not traded actively in the retail market. You can also choose debt mutual funds for tax efficient returns with high liquidity.'* We'll discuss mutual funds in more detail in the next chapter.

That said, be forewarned that investing in bonds does not mean cutting out all of your risk. Bonds come with a fair number of associated risks owing to fluctuations in interest rates, company defaults and the possibility of rating agencies downgrading companies.

STEP 4

Investing in mutual funds

IF I ASK YOU WHAT COMES TO YOUR MIND WHEN YOU HEAR THE term 'mutual funds' I am sure the first thing that pops into your head is a combination of vague images signifying growth and prosperity, with the 'mutual funds are subject to market risk' disclaimer being recited in a frenzied tone as its background score.

Quite obviously then, the subject of mutual funds remains clouded in mystery for most people, who perceive them to be a risky asset, which is quite contradictory to our view of them as a smart alternative for investment.

A mutual fund is actually a professionally managed portfolio of stocks and securities that pools money from investors to purchase securities. As an investor, you own units representing the portion of the fund that you hold, which is based upon the amount that you have invested. This is why an investor is also referred to as a unit holder. The ***Net Asset Value*** (NAV) of a mutual fund represents the market value of each unit of a fund. In other words, this is the price at which you can buy or sell units of the fund.

Most mutual funds are 'open-ended', which means that, as an investor you can buy or sell shares (directly or through a distributor) of the fund at any time. Generally, you can get your money back within three working days. Any increase in value of your investment, along with other income earned, is passed on to you in proportion with the number of units you own after deducting applicable expenses and taxes.

Contrary to popular perception, you can reduce your risk by investing in a mutual fund. As it invests across various equity and debt securities, it is considered to be a trade-off between returns and risk.

- The NAV is calculated daily, based upon the combined market value of the shares, bonds and securities held by a fund on that particular day but it doesn't fluctuate throughout the day like the value of a stock.
- Also, unlike a stock price which might remain unaffected by dividends that its company gives out, when a mutual fund scheme pays a dividend, the total value of the scheme is reduced, so the NAV also gets reduced proportionately.
- Just like the stock prices, the NAV helps you keep track of how a mutual fund is doing. If its value rises, then it means that the value of its investments are rising, whereas if the value falls then it means that the value of its investments are also falling.

- The Association of Mutual Funds in India (AMFI) is an independent association that oversees the functioning of the mutual fund industry with the aim of safeguarding the interests of investors and fund houses alike. The NAVs of all mutual fund schemes are published on the AMFI website and on each of the fund company websites every day. It is important to know this to ensure that you are up-to-date about your investments.

What are the different types of mutual funds you can invest in?

Equity Mutual Funds

When you invest in an equity fund, you do not buy the actual stock – the fund does it for you. These funds give you no assurance on the principal, rate of interest or tenure of your investment. Since this is an equity-linked instrument it is subject to market risks, and compared to debt mutual funds it is more risky. Usually a greater risk component also signals greater rewards but if a company offers ridiculously high returns, it is a sure indication that something might be off. Remember, if something looks too good to be true, it probably isn't.

Equity funds not only have the potential to deliver high returns, but also diversify their investments in different companies across a number of different industry sectors to counter risk.

WHAT THE EXPERTS SAY

'Indian retail investors can invest in government securities; however, there has not been much appetite to invest directly. The main issue is liquidity and large lot sizes which make it difficult for lay investors to benefit from this investment. Mostly investors take the mutual fund route while investing in government securities since they offer liquidity. Mutual funds which invest in government securities are known as gilt funds. However, all investments in mutual funds are subject to market risks and, therefore, there is always a small amount of risk, however negligible.'

– **Suresh Soni**
CEO, Deutsche Asset Management India Pvt. Ltd

Hybrid Funds

As the name suggests, hybrid funds have a combination of asset classes in their portfolio. They invest in a hybrid mix of debt, money market instruments and equities. ***Balanced funds*** are hybrid funds that aim to find a balance between growth and income by investing in stocks as well as debt in a ratio of sixty to forty, more or less.

Index Funds

These are schemes that invest in stocks that are part of an index, like the Sensex or the Nifty. They do not invest in stocks outside of the indices.

Sector Funds

Sector funds also invest in equities, but specifically in one or two market sectors only. For example, they might invest in the automobile sector, or in banking stocks, or in pharmaceuticals.

Liquid Funds

Liquid funds provide easy liquidity. They help preserve your capital and give you a moderate income, too. Liquid funds exclusively invest in safer short-term instruments like certificates of deposit, commercial paper and government securities. Returns on these schemes fluctuate less as compared to other funds and are, therefore, ideal if you are looking to park your money for a relatively short period.

Equity-Linked Savings Scheme

An equity-linked savings scheme (ELSS) is a type of mutual fund scheme but it works a little differently from other mutual funds in terms of investment period and taxation. The basic difference is that money in an ELSS gets locked in for a period of three years but any amount invested in this, up to a limit of one lakh, is tax deductible. The minimum investment is ₹500 and you can invest in a lump sum or through an SIP (Systematic Investment Plan).

ELSS schemes invest in the stock market so the usual rules of risk and volatility will apply. However, with a three-year lock-in period, you are giving yourself a chance to ride an entire investment cycle. This is a great investment option if you are willing to take a little risk.

Fixed Maturity Plans

These are also a little different from other mutual funds since they are essentially close-ended schemes with a wide fixed maturity period ranging from as short as 15 days to as long as two years. By close-ended we mean that you cannot exit this fund before the notified period. Fixed Maturity Plans (FMPs) invest in various fixed income instruments – bonds, government securities, money market instruments and so on. A good source of diversification, they are a low-risk investment, and, therefore, the returns from it are also not very high We would suggest you do not go for these if you are looking for long-term wealth creation.

A majority of Indian women investors will naturally veer towards investing in mutual funds because they have been advised by friends or family that stock-picking is too risky and it is far better to have a professional manage your money. Well, yes and no. As we've said before, you do need to have a stomach for stock-picking but hopefully, by now, you have begun to think about stocks from a more informed point-of-view. And while there are benefits to having a professional fund manager work for you, we want, once again, to caution you to stay in the driver's seat.

MONEYSMART ALERT!

- Income received for units of a mutual fund specified under Section 10 (23D) of the Income Tax Act are exempt from income tax in India, but the mutual funds need to pay the distribution tax in debt-oriented schemes.[5]
- Mutual funds held for a period of 12 months or more are categorized as long-term assets and the sale of these at a profit will be taxed as long-term capital gains. Any sale in a period of less than 12 months would, however, attract the usual rates on the profit of sale.

Understanding Exchange Traded Funds (ETFs)

An Exchange Traded Fund is different from a mutual fund, even though both primarily do the same thing. Unlike a mutual fund, the units of which need to be bought and sold at the counter of the mutual fund company, an ETF is an index fund that is listed and traded on exchanges, just like stocks. Basically, it's a type or class of mutual fund that passively invests in a basket of securities – equities, bonds or commodities – against which units are issued by the fund and such units can only be traded through designated stock exchanges where the ETF is listed.

The first ETF was launched in 1993 in the United States of America.

How do ETFs work?

An ETF is essentially a basket of stocks that reflects the composition of an index, like the Nifty or the BSE Sensex. The proportion in which the ETF allocates money to a stock may or may not be the same as individual stocks' weight in the index. Like mutual funds, ETFs have a NAV, but as ETFs trade in real time, funds provide an indicative NAV, or iNAV, which is the real-time NAV of an ETF. The iNAV may be different from the market price. It is based upon the NAV of its underlying stocks.

Unlike a regular mutual fund, where you can buy a fraction of the unit, ETFs are available in multiples of units. If you are buying a large lot size of say ₹15 to 20 lakh or more, you can even approach the fund house directly.

ETFs provide you with a great opportunity to invest your money in overseas stock markets, in different countries across different sectors. So if you are interested in exposing your investment portfolio to the global market, ETFs are the perfect investment for you.

Rikesh Mirchandani, the CEO of Ocean City Capital, says there are many advantages of investing in ETFs over equities, bonds and commodities. '*One of the greatest advantages is that investing in ETFs provides diversification by investing in a portfolio of stocks. The portfolio of an equity-based ETF can be constructed in many ways, such as to replicate market indices existing in a country – like Sensex/Nifty-based ETFs in India. Or it could be constructed on the economies of groups such as BRIC ETFs. Another thing is that bonds and commodities primarily trade only through wholesale markets and are generally out of reach of retail investors. However, ETFs have made it possible for them to add fixed income assets and commodities to their investment portfolios, thereby allowing them to diversify their risk.*' However, he cautions, '*One thing to be mindful of is tracking errors, which is the most common reason of the under-performance of an ETF compared to its corresponding market index. Essentially, what happens in this situation is that an ETF fund falls short of tracking the index movements and returns.*'

As such, ETFs are ideal if you are looking for a short-term investment option.

KEY POINTS TO REMEMBER

- The minimum investment for an ETF is one unit.
- You can easily buy or sell an ETF just like any other stock on the exchange or directly with the fund house.
- The fund will create or redeem units only in predefined lot sizes in exchange for a predefined portfolio basket. You can also pay cash directly to the fund through a 'cash subscription' method.
- The expense ratio (a measure of operating cost) of an ETF is typically lower than many other investment options.

- Do watch out for transaction fees – remember, you pay a transaction fee every time you trade units.
- You can place limit orders on the ETFs.
- ETFs are highly liquid, and unlike many close-ended mutual funds, ETFs trade very closely to their NAV because their portfolio holdings are transparent.

The Perfect Timing

The first question that probably comes to your mind when you decide to invest your money is: '*Is this the best time to put my money in this asset?*' Anyone who has invested or has thought of investing her money has had to grapple with the question of perfect timing. According to our experts, this is one of the trickiest questions to answer. Leo Puri, Managing Director of UTI Asset Management, says that market timing – buying low and selling high – is easier said than done. According to him, the notion that life can be understood backwards but has to be lived forwards is applicable to the capital markets as well. What you require in effect is a systematic approach to investment – you should invest across categories as well as in assets with varying maturity periods to have diversification in asset-classes and also in holding periods, ensuring that you have some access to capital at one point or another.

Buying when everyone is despondently selling, and selling when everyone is buying requires great mental fortitude and pays the greatest reward. But an 'empathy gap' prevents us from doing so. If you are thinking of investing in a mutual fund then there is a very viable solution to this problem and that is a Systematic Investment Plan (SIP). An SIP is a system in which you apportion a regular amount of your income into mutual fund investments each month rather than putting down a lump sum. An SIP forces you to invest across the cycles of a market and inculcates a discipline in your investments. There are a couple of reasons to do this.

Firstly, not everyone has a large amount of cash at their disposal to invest each month. Also, you have to remember that markets can be volatile – things are fine if you invested your money at the low end of the market, but if you put your money in at the peak you are not going to be a happy camper when it falls (unless, of course, you have a long-term horizon). Committing a regular amount each month doesn't mean you have to break the bank – you can apportion as much as ₹5,000 per month. For many people, that's less than what they spend on restaurant bills.

WHAT THE EXPERTS SAY

'The holding period of any investment depends on your financial goal. A minimum investment holding period should be there to fit in with your portfolio; this holding period should suit your goals and mutual fund products. Depending on your financial needs, the portfolio could consist of buckets – a bucket of liquid and ultra-short-term funds, another of short-term funds, and perhaps one with long-term debt funds and equity. How much one should allot to ultra-short-term, short-term and long-term depends upon your needs and the timing of your needs. The mode of exiting the fund also depends upon your financial goals. However, if you wish, you can aggregate your redemption by redeeming units at specified intervals – monthly, quarterly, etc., either on your own or by choosing a Systematic Withdrawal Plan (SWP).'

– **Leo Puri**

Managing Director, UTI Asset Management Company

How do you measure the risk of mutual funds?

It's a good idea to know about some statistical indicators of investment risk that are used to analyse stocks, bonds and mutual fund portfolios. Historically, these statistical measures have been used to predict investment risk or volatility and help in assessing the performance of equity, fixed-income and mutual fund investments by comparing them to market benchmarks.

These are alpha, beta, r-squared, standard deviation and the sharpe ratio. All these are indicated on the mutual fund fact-sheet in Appendix 2a on p. 297.

Alpha

Alpha measures your investment's performance on a risk-adjusted basis or, as Himanshu Kohli of Client Associates puts it, '*Your fund manager's ability to beat the benchmark.*' It compares the volatility (price-risk) of your security or fund portfolio to a benchmark index. Any excess in your investment return as compared to the return of the benchmark index is known as its alpha.

Simply put, a positive alpha of 1.0 means the fund has outperformed its benchmark index by 1%. That would be a good indicator that your investment manager is doing well for you, whereas an alpha of –1% means that your portfolio is underperforming the market by 1%. '*The more positive the alpha, the better your investment portfolio as your fund manager is able to get better returns than the benchmark*,' says Kohli.

Beta

Beta measures the volatility or risk of a security or a portfolio as compared to the market as a whole. By definition, the market has a beta of 1.0. Individual securities and portfolio values are measured to see how much they deviate from this market measure, a lower beta being preferable to a higher beta.

So a beta of 1.0 means that your investment's price will move in line with the market. A beta of less than 1.0 means that your investment will be less volatile than the market, and a beta of more than 1.0 means your investment's price will be more volatile than the market. For example, if your fund portfolio's beta is 1.2, it's theoretically 20% more volatile than the market.

R-Squared

R-Squared is a statistical measure that represents the percentage of your fund portfolio's movements that can be explained by movements in a benchmark index.

R-squared values range from 0 to 100. A mutual fund with an r-squared value between 85 and 100 means its performance record is closely correlated to the index but a fund rated 70 or less would not perform like the index.

Standard Deviation

This is a measure of risk or volatility of a portfolio. Particularly volatile securities with a higher standard deviation are considered a higher risk because their performance can change quickly in either direction and at any moment.

The standard deviation of a fund measures this risk by measuring the degree to which the fund fluctuates in relation to its mean return or the average return of a fund over a period.

For example, a fund that has a consistent four-year return of 3% would have a mean, or average, of 3%. The standard deviation for this fund would then be zero because the fund's return in any given year does not differ from its four-year mean.

But say you have a choice between two stocks: Stock A historically returns 10% with a standard deviation of 5% and Stock B has a 10% return and carries a standard deviation of 2%. Which one is more risky?

Stock A has the potential to earn 5% more than the expected return, but is equally likely to earn 5% less than the expected return. Likewise, Stock B can vary by up to 2%.

So from a risk and return perspective, Stock B is less risky than Stock A.

The bottom line is that a lower standard deviation is more optimal, because the closer you are to the mean, the more you are maximizing the return received for the risk acquired.

Sharpe Ratio

This measures risk-adjusted performance.

The sharpe ratio tells you whether your investment's returns are due to wise investment decisions or whether they are simply a result of excess risk. This measurement is very useful because although your portfolio or security can yield higher returns than its peers, it is a good investment only as long as those higher returns do not carry too much additional risk.

The greater an investment's sharpe ratio, the better its risk-adjusted performance.

Expense Ratio

This extremely important measure shows you how much the mutual fund scheme is charging you for assets under management. So an expense ratio of 1% for a ₹100 scheme means that you will pay a rupee for your assets worth ₹100. The lower the expense ratio, obviously, the better off you are. Typically, for fixed income, expense ratios should be around 1%, whereas for equities it should be 1.5 to 2%.

Past Performance

In one year your fund might give you a 10% return, whereas in three years it might give you a 30% return. What is important though, is to look at a compounded annual growth rate rather than an absolute or simple return, annual growth which is compounded on an annual basis. For example, if your return compounded on a three-year basis is 10% and the benchmark index return is 8%, you know your fund is doing well.

Credit Rating

This is the credit rating of debt securities. So a rating of AAA indicates a debt security of the highest rating.

Average Maturity

This shows the average number of years until the bond or fund matures.

Sector Exposure

This measure shows how much of your portfolio lies in each sector of the industry.

By now you're probably thinking, 'This is a lot of information! How on earth am I going to remember it all?' Well the good news is that you don't have to; not all of it in one go anyway. Just remember that this is a handy reference that you can come back to any time you find yourself wondering how to decode your monthly mutual fund fact sheet. If you look at it regularly enough, we'll bet our last rupee that you'll internalize the information very soon.

Your Money Mantra

Bear in mind four key points with regard to mutual funds that will make the difference when you plan your portfolio.

- The more you earn, the more you save and the sooner you start saving.
- Never invest any securities that are not regulated or are under-regulated. If any asset promises too-good-to-be-true returns, chances that are there might be something off and further investigation is warranted.
- Mutual funds offer you the opportunity to invest in a basket of debt, equity or government securities rather than in single stocks or bonds, navigating your risk for you.
- An SIP is a great opportunity for you to inculcate the investing habit without putting too much pressure on your monthly budget.

Illiquid Investments

INVESTING OUTSIDE THE BOX

'I would look at alternative assets for two reasons – overall diversification and providing a negative correlation to traditional asset classes. Research has shown that these could do well when the performance of other assets is not up to the mark. Alternate investments are a better choice than hedge funds and PE [Private Equity] funds where the ticket prices are high and your money is held up for 10 years or more.'

– **Amit Jeffrey**
Asset Allocation Manager, Client Associates

STEP 1

Liquidity: it's got nothing to do with water or beverages

SO FAR, WE'VE LARGELY TALKED ABOUT LIQUID INVESTMENTS. In other words, investments that can be easily liquidated or turned into cash. However, as you sharpen your investing skills, you'll find that there are plenty of other kinds of investments that might yield a higher return as long as you are willing to hold on to them for a while.

Typical examples accessible to the Indian woman include alternatives like gold, property, and art and antiques.

Investing in alternative assets

When it comes to understanding alternative assets, the first thing to know is that there is no fixed definition as to what this asset class is. Every financial house appears to have its own definition, which often conveniently includes investment instruments that cannot be classified elsewhere.

Amit Jeffrey, Asset Allocation Manager at Client Associates, an investment management company, provided us with the perfect definition: '*Alternative assets form an asset class that provides an alternative to a traditional asset class – traditional asset classes being debt, equity and cash.*'

He also told us that the risk-return profile of alternative assets that you invest in should be totally different from that of traditional asset classes. How else will you succeed in diversifying your portfolio?

Putting this into context, he further explained, '*When you invest in equities, you are looking to do so for a longer term, say 3 years or more, so that you can get a 15–16% return on an annual basis. For debt, you are looking at 7–8% annual returns, but when it comes to alternate asset classes there is no such fixed threshold. Your returns can vary – it can be north of 20% and it can come with higher or lower risk.*'

Just as you can invest in equities directly through the stock market or through an equities mutual fund, you can also invest directly in alternate assets or through an alternative asset mutual fund.

If you decide to invest directly then bear in mind that most alternative asset classes are not necessarily traded on an exchange. This is because many of them are non-financial in nature. So you can trade commodities like gold and silver on an exchange but you cannot trade real estate on an exchange (in other countries, this is possible through a mechanism called a Real Estate Investment Trust or REIT, but this type of investment is still at a nascent stage in India).

If you decide to take the mutual fund route, it is important to note that the underlying investments in the alternative fund can comprise of non-financial assets such as commodities or real assets like real estate, a coal mine or any other natural resources. They can also consist of non-traditional financial assets like long-short funds.

Types of alternative assets

The following are some of the alternative assets you can invest in:

Property

Investing in property means buying a hard asset like a piece of land, an apartment or a house, or even investing in commercial retail outlets. Since we've dedicated an entire chapter to this topic, we won't talk much about it here.

Financial Assets

Investing in financial assets can mean investing in funds derived from equity- or debt-based products. However, they are structured in a totally different manner. An example of this category would be ***long-short funds***. Long-short funds are mutual funds that offer trading strategies which are typically employed by a hedge fund for regular investors like you and me. Unlike most mutual funds, these are considered alternative investments that use various strategies to maximize your returns, regardless of the market's position. While it's good to be aware of the different kinds of alternate assets out there, this one is more suited for an experienced investor.

You can also invest in other financial assets like ***hedge funds***, ***private equity*** and ***venture capital funds***.[1] But these are primarily suited for high net-worth individuals rather than amateur investors. You can discuss these assets with your investment advisor, but remember they are strategies that require you to take a directional view of the markets. It is not something you will be familiar with during your early days of investing.

High net-worth individuals are those who have investable assets of US $1 million or about ₹6 crore.

Commodities

Commodities form the heart of market activity in India and have been around for hundreds of years, long before equity markets. For this reason alone, it's worth exploring this area.

As the operational manager of the household, the Indian woman has traditionally been responsible for the purchase of food and groceries. When you think about it, buying commodities is sort of an extension of this idea.

Let us suppose you had a store of, say, sesame seeds at home during a time when supply was low in the market, you could sell them to the next household or to a middleman willing to pay a higher price for them because he, in turn, would sell them to an oil-making company. In a nutshell, that's what buying and selling commodities is about.

India being a traditionally agricultural economy has had local mandis for most agricultural commodities – for example, soya is sold in Indore, castor seeds are sold in Ahmedabad and cotton in Surendranagar. It is also the largest consumer of gold in the world, which naturally means a huge market for this precious metal, largely based in Mumbai. Until recently, however, these commodity markets had only a regional presence for the physical trade of the particular commodity. But now the country has seen the development of national commodity exchanges similar to the Bombay Stock Exchange (BSE) and the National Stock Exchange (NSE) that specifically deal in commodity derivatives in an electronic trading environment.

Wider reach obviously means wider participation. So a wholesaler of castor seeds now has a wider customer base available to him beyond those who show up at the mandi in Ahmedabad. The price he can get is then based not just on the local demand-supply conditions but also on the global demand and supply.

The various categories of commodities are:

- Precious metals, such as gold, silver, diamond, platinum
- Industrial metals, such as copper, zinc, lead
- Minerals, such as coal, bauxite, iron ore
- Agricultural goods, such as wheat, corn, cotton, oils, oilseeds
- Soft commodities, such as coffee, cocoa, sugar
- Livestock, such as live cattle, pigs, poultry
- Energy, such as crude oil, natural gas, gasoline.

Why invest in commodities at all?

The biggest advantage of investing in commodities is diversification. Also, the fact that you can invest in cyclical patterns based upon the seasonality of some of the commodities, to advantageous results.

You can invest in commodities by creating a demat account through a commodities broker. This is separate from your equities demat account. Essentially, you would require separate demat accounts for different investment options and you would invest through a commodities exchange.

Commodity Exchanges in India

1. Multi Commodity Exchange of India Ltd, Mumbai (MCX) (www.mcxindia.com)
2. National Commodity and Derivative Exchange, Mumbai (NCDEX) (www.ncdex.com)
3. National Multi-Commodity Exchange of India Ltd, Ahmedabad (NMCE) (www.nmce.com)
4. National Board of Trade, Indore (NBOT) (www.nbotind.org)

It must be said that currently there are more institutional players than retail players who operate via commodity exchanges, but if you know a thing or two about commodities and are willing to do your research on price movements in the global market, then you can certainly buy and sell on the exchanges directly.

Just as SEBI regulates the stock market, the Forward Markets Commission (FMC) regulates the commodities market.

Before you invest in commodities, though, the one thing to consider is the 'other side' of the equation.

While investing in commodities might prove to be worth every paisa, it might also drive up the price of food. This would work in your favour as an investor because you can profit from the situation, but it works against you as a consumer.

You need to consider the reality of the food equation and figure out what will have a greater impact on you and your household – the availability of food versus the value of your investment. Food safety activists are intrinsically against the notion of speculating on food-based commodities as they believe that it drives inflation.

'In the 2007–08 world food crises, one of the driving forces behind higher food prices were speculators,' says Rajeev Patel, food activist and author of *Stuffed and Starved: The Hidden Battle for the World Food System. 'Speculators bought food because they knew its price would rise, holding on to it until they could sell it for more than what they paid for it. India has had a sad history with this kind of speculation. Nobel prize-winning economist Amartya Sen studied the Bengal famine and found that there was plenty of food even as the poor died of hunger. The reason: hoarders betting on higher prices. So if you're thinking of investing in food, or in a commodities index in which food plays a part, think twice. Many reputable banks have stepped away from the practise because it can hurt people who can barely afford to eat.'*

Art, Antiques and Collectibles

There is a growing investment market for art, antiques and collectibles as many of these items are of immense value, which increases as the items get older. Even though the art market in India is burgeoning and the country is a ripe storehouse for collectibles like rare stamps, documents, rare editions of books and antiques, the market for these items is extremely fragmented. Unlike other countries, Indian portfolio managers do not have a clear understanding of how these items can qualify as an asset class. Hence, they tend to brush them off as hobby items which do not have serious potential as investment.

Like any asset class, the key to investing in these items is to familiarize yourself with what is available to you at what value, think about what price they can fetch in the future and assets whether they can fetch that price with minimal logistical hassle. This is particularly important for assets that are physical in nature.

Here are some categories to consider:

- Art
- Rare books
- Rare stamps and documents
- Rare coins
- Antiques
- Wine
- Other collectibles

In this book, we will discuss the art market in detail because there has been actual activity in this area even though the price points can often fall beyond the reach of the lay investor. That said, having some cursory information can help you plan for the future. As you increase your net wealth, you can work your way to investing in this asset class, too.

Your Money Mantra

The alternative asset class lies on the other end of the investment spectrum. It offers options removed from traditional assets and is a great choice for any investor who wants to tap the potential of her money.

- It provides you with the benefit of diversification.
- It has a negative relation with other traditional assets like equities. Therefore, it acts as a financial buffer.
- When investing in alternative assets, you should compare the risks with the return. You should understand that these assets could be illiquid as well. Be ready to have your money tied up for at least five years.

STEP 2

Investing in gold

SUDHA DID NOT HAVE A PROPER INVESTMENT PORTFOLIO UNTIL 2007. Until then, she had allocated some portion of her savings to buying gold jewellery. '*I'm not a wage-earner, so I had to be even more cautious about my budget. Anything left at the end of the month would go to some small gold purchase – sometimes a pendant, sometimes a pair of earrings.*'

Over the years, Sudha had collected a sizeable portfolio of gold, but because it was hidden away in the safety of a bank locker she didn't really think of it as an investment.

'*Then, in 2007, when everyone was talking about the success of the equity markets I thought it's high time I started too. I decided to start small – I sold two lakhs worth of my gold jewellery to buy equities and added another three lakhs in cash for a total equity investment of five lakhs. It was the year I hoped to become savvier about investing – I was counting on the fact that great things would happen for me,*' she recalls.

That year Sudha learned more about investing than she had bargained for.

'*By the end of 2008, my equity holdings were down by more than 50%. I was so upset to have lost all that money! But then the price of gold sky-rocketed. Everything I had in the locker was worth much more that year. I was glad that I had collected it and cursed myself for having divested two lakhs' worth to buy equities.*'

As we know from previous discussions on market upswings and downswings, the equities market did eventually recover and so did Sudha's portfolio. But in 2008, she wouldn't have known that – she was just relieved to have kept most of her wealth in gold.

'*Gold is a safe haven. If you see fear flooding the market or if you see currency depreciation at any time, it is always accompanied by the acquisition of gold and a rise in gold prices*,' says Chirag Mehta, Senior Fund Manager at Quantum Asset Management Ltd. '*Gold diversifies your portfolio and it's always good to have it [make up] 10–20% of your total portfolio because it's like having spare cash. In 2008, in India, equities were down by more than 50% but gold was up by more than 30%.*'

Clearly, the gold Sudha had in her portfolio compensated for a large portion of her losses.

So what about silver? Sudha had collected a little bit of that, too, but unfortunately its value didn't rise in the same way as that of its yellow-metal counterpart.

'*Even though it is a precious metal which has high value, silver acts very differently from gold*,' says Mehta. '*It is regarded more as an industrial commodity, and 65–70% of it goes towards industrial use. Given this, you will typically see it perform well when the global economy does well. This is why silver didn't do as well during the financial crisis in 2008 and the months thereafter.*'

Sudha had also considered putting her money in platinum, which was frequently talked about among her friends but since she didn't know enough about it, she decided not to venture in that direction.

> The Indian woman has long had an emotional relationship with gold. According to the world gold council, Indian women own more gold than the entire US Treasury – about 18,000 tonnes of gold compared to the US national gold reserve's 8,600 tonnes![1]

Why gold has such a strong hold on Indians is a question of great complexity. Gold binds ties that are deeply embedded in our culture. All our major life events are accompanied by the giving of gold – weddings, naming ceremonies, even a child's first meal of solid food.

For the longest time, gold jewellery was the only real asset that the Indian woman had access to. As the decision-makers in household matters, women have traditionally been well aware that buying gold jewellery is a smart move, given that gold is an asset that yields financial gains.

Gold purchases are considered auspicious during certain festivals. In rural India, purchasing gold has traditionally been linked to the outcome of the monsoons.

Satyajit Das, a former investment banker and author of *Extreme Money: The Masters of the Universe and the Cult of Risk*, believes that the reason why Indian women love gold is because '*it's portable and is probably the only thing that Indian women can truly consider theirs. Also, it can be used as collateral for loans*.'

The massive shift to consumerism around gold is, however, a recent phenomenon. Back in 1982, India consumed only 65 tonnes of gold and up to 1990 imports were practically banned. However, after deregulation, gold purchases sky-rocketed. As domestic inflation soared, Indians began to look beyond the borders of the country to purchase gold. Much of the foreign gold that comes into India does so through banks, and although back in the day loans against gold collateral were typically given by moneylenders, today they are offered by registered financial firms as well.

GOLD – GREAT COLLATERAL FOR A LOAN

If you need to get a loan for education or to buy a car, your gold jewellery might be an excellent way to fund such a loan. Jewellery that is lying idle in your bank locker can be pledged to get a loan. All leading banks in the country provide quick loans against gold jewellery for varying amounts. For example, ICICI offers gold loans up to ₹15 lakh and Kotak Mahindra offers loans up to 90% of the gold's value.

All that glitters is not gold

Buying, gifting and wearing gold jewellery may be auspicious but it isn't necessarily the best investment decision.

- Gold jewellery is actually less pure than brick gold and more prone to damage because of the wear and tear involved. So even though the value of gold as a metal may have risen since you purchased the piece of jewellery, if you decide to sell it, you may find that your piece of jewellery has depreciated in value.
- The making charges you pay while purchasing a piece of jewellery are not compensated when you sell it. Plus, you must consider the fact that the piece of jewellery you are

trying to sell might not be in fashion, which will further lessen its value.

- Jewellery add-ons like precious stones typically increase the weight but rarely increase the value, and only select jewellers will buy back a piece of jewellery if it yields a depreciated value.

All these factors make selling gold jewellery a somewhat losing proposition.

Alternatively, you could buy gold coins or bullion. The value of gold coins and bars does not typically lessen due to usage and wastage. You can buy gold in its purest forms in the bullion market and find that it yields profitable returns based upon the actual price of gold.

Compare a gold chain of 15 grams with a gold coin of 15 grams, both bought at the same time. Assuming the price of gold has risen a year later, the gold coin will definitely yield more for various reasons – it is 24 carat gold, as opposed to the chain, which would be 22 or 23 carat gold. (To make even the finest jewellery, it is impossible to use 24 carat gold as it is too soft.) Even so, the gold chain would have been purchased at a higher price because you would have paid making charges for it.

Bullion India is a great gold e-trader which enables you to make secure investments in small denominations of physical gold online.[3] You can also opt to have the bars or coins of gold delivered to your doorstep.

Satyajit Das, however, doesn't quite agree that gold is an ideal investment tool. '*Gold does not pay interest or dividends,*' he says. '*Essentially, you are relying on the price of the commodity which could go up or down at any time. For example, if you bought gold*

India buys around 40% of the world's gold and most of that quantity is consumed by Indian women. Even though in 2013, China outpaced India for the first time ever in terms of pure gold purchases, India still possesses more than half of the gold that is in China.

in the last three years, you would have been on a rocky road as there have been a few dips in the price of the metal. However, if you purchased it 10 years ago, then you would have done well as the overall price has increased from less than ₹10,000 per 10 grams in 2004 to ₹30,000 per 10 grams in 2014.'

A word about when to actually buy gold: aside from festive occasions, the one time you don't want to buy gold, especially jewellery, in India is in the thick of the wedding season. Why? For the simple reason that you will be in a long line with everyone else and the jewellers will charge extra just because they know they can!

Is investing in gold better than investing in a fixed deposit?

As Satyajit Das points out, gold might not pay interest like your fixed deposit or dividends like bonds do, so you may ask: why bother investing in gold instead of in a fixed deposit where you can actually see and measure your returns?

It all comes back to the idea of your real rate of return, which we mentioned in Section 3. Have you taken into account inflation and are you absolutely sure that you are not, in fact, getting negative returns on your fixed deposit? Remember, when interest rates are lower than the increase in your cost of living then your earnings from fixed income instruments will not be able to keep pace with your increased expenses, leading to negative returns.

The difference with gold is that it's a time-tested asset that holds value over the long term. Fixed deposits are great short-term investments but in the long run they can give you negative returns. Gold, on the other hand, is historically known to keep pace with inflation, preserving the purchasing power of your capital.

WHAT THE EXPERTS SAY

'Women in India have had a traditional relationship with gold. It has been their safety blanket. They have always purchased it in the form of jewellery and used it as a financial tool only in case of severe exigencies.

Today, there are a lot of opportunities for investing in gold. Exchange traded funds and gold mutual funds invest in gold without the difficulty of physically owning and storing it. Additionally, for those who already own gold, a few banks and NBFCs offer gold deposits and even loans against gold.

These financial products provide women flexibility in investing in and divesting gold.'

– **Naina Lal Kidwai**

Group General Manager and Country Head, HSBC India

Gold and Silver Indices

The Gold and Silver Indices (GSI) compare the movement of physical gold and silver in India vis-a-vis the Nifty. The price of physical gold and silver in India is not only dependent on international prices but also on the Indian rupee.

You cannot trade on the GSI but you can use it to understand how gold and silver prices are doing compared to the stock markets.

Investing in GETFs

Unlike the days gone by, today, you can hold gold exchange traded funds (GETFs), as we discussed earlier. A GETF is an ETF that tracks the price of gold.

GETFs are typically open-ended gold funds whose units represent physical gold that is 99.5% pure, with each unit representing 1 gram of gold.

Why is this called paper gold? Because just like stocks, you don't actually 'hold' the gold, yet you get to participate in the bullion market through your ownership represented by the fraction of gold you own in the ETF. In other words, you can buy gold in the form of paper units.

Like all other ETFs, gold ETFs are listed on the stock exchange and are traded on a daily basis. So you can imagine that owning gold in this format is much more liquid and logistically easier than owning gold jewellery or bullion. Some ETFs invest in the metal itself while others give you exposure to gold, using instruments linked to its prices, such as gold futures or derivatives.

Even though GETFs are slowly becoming more mainstream in the Indian investing scenario, women still prefer to hold on to physical gold rather than purchasing paper gold. Chirag Mehta, Senior Fund Manager, Alternative Investments, Quantum Asset Management Ltd. says this is because of a lack of awareness of the price efficiencies of GETFs: '*Even though the Indian woman is extremely price sensitive, she doesn't realize that when she buys physical gold, she is paying anywhere between 5–20% more than she would if she bought gold through an ETF.*'

For years, you have been buying small amounts of gold in the form of a pendant or earrings, bargaining as much as you can to get the lowest price and then continuing this pattern to collect more and more over a period of time. What you haven't realized is that the smaller the amount of physical gold the higher the price you've paid for it per unit, because factored into it were the price of gold, the making charges, and wholesale and retail premiums. Whereas, if you buy even 0.5 grams of gold through a GETF, you will get it at a purely wholesale price.

It makes sense, doesn't it? You no longer need to worry about theft or locker charges. '*When you invest in an ETF, your gold is completely safe, kept in a secured vault with complete assurance*,' says Chirag Mehta. The only difference is that now you are buying gold through your demat account and broker rather than buying it at the bazaar.

Since GETFs exactly reflect the price of gold, their value will move up and down with the price of gold. So if you look at the price of gold on a chart, it will reflect the performance of your investment in a GETF portfolio.

Why does investing in a GETF work out cheaper than buying physical gold?

You might be wondering how this is possible given that a GETF actually represents physical gold.

Remember, when you buy jewellery you are subject to making charges, storage charges, and you can lose a good 25–30% on re-sale. Even with bullion, you cannot escape storage costs. With GETFs, you simply pay the entry fee, the brokerage charge of about 1% and an annual fee of about 1%.

Of course, if the ETF declares a dividend, you will be subject to a dividend distribution tax. However, it's important to note that a gold ETF that simply tracks the price of the precious metal will not usually pay dividends because the purpose of this fund is to simply buy and hold the gold.

A gold mining fund, on the other hand, is more likely to give dividends.

WHAT THE EXPERTS SAY

'In India, we tend to buy gold on festive occasions or special life occasions such as for a daughter's marriage. The great thing about investing in a gold ETF is that it allows you to accumulate gold units over the years. By doing this, you lock the price of gold. Yet, when you want to make gold ornaments at the time of your daughter's wedding, you can encash the units and and get the jewellery made according to your preferences. Of course, you will incur some making charges, but why pay those making charges now for a design that you may or may not like 10 years from now.'

– **Swati Kulkarni**

Executive Vice President and Fund Manager, UTI Asset Management Company (P) Ltd

Satyajit Das adds words of warning that GETFs come with the risk of default by the financial institution you buy them from, just like stocks and bonds issued by a company. '*Even when funds are invested in physical gold, the metal is held by custodians, exposing them to failure of these entities*,' he says.

A number of major financial services firms offer gold ETFs – Axis, Goldman Sachs, HDFC, ICICI Prudential and more.

For a comprehensive list of GETFs on the NSE, refer to Appendix 2. If you have an online trading account, you can directly buy the ETFs online or your broker can easily buy them for you.

Your Money Mantra

If you are considering alternative assets to diversify your portfolio, then gold is a sound choice. It might not be an investment in the sense that it does not give immediate returns, but compared to other more traditional investment choices (like fixed deposits), it has a better chance of keeping up with inflation.

- Gold is easy to liquidate. It can also act as collateral in case you need to take a loan.
- Gold jewellery is not the best form of investment as its value may not increase to the levels you expect.
- It is always advisable to buy gold in the form of bullion or GETFs to save on storage costs and avoid depreciation.

STEP 3

Investing in property

EVEN THOUGH INDIA IS A MASSIVE COUNTRY, IT DOESN'T HAVE an unending supply of land. In fact, given the growth rate of our population so far, it is highly likely that we are going to face a scarcity of land to house our population in the not-so-distant future. Already, Indian companies have acquired land on foreign shores, as cultivable land at home is rapidly losing out to urbanization, industry and infrastructure projects.

India's cities are also growing at a rapid pace thanks to urban migration. According to Rajesh Krishnan, CEO, Brick Eagle Investments, a developer of affordable housing, roughly half a million people came to Mumbai each year to make a living. '*The city is annually growing at a pace of 10 to 15,000 acres. Panvel was a relatively quite suburb until a few years ago but today it is no different from the rest of the city, with huge traffic jams and congested spaces.*'

Essentially, what you are faced with is a double-edged sword. As the country continues to urbanize and bring more housing and commercial property to the market, it gives you more options in terms of where you can choose to live and work and invest your money.

Again, as land becomes more and more scarce, the price of property rises. This works out to be expensive if you are not a property owner, but if you are it can be a massive source of wealth.

According to the United Nations, 843 million people will reside in Indian cities by 2050. That's equivalent to the combined population of the US, Brazil, Russia, Japan and Germany. The UN also says that more than 300 million will be added to India's working age population by the same year. This is the highest rate of change for urban population among the BRIC nations (Brazil, Russia, India and China).[4]

Who doesn't want to own a home? In India, as elsewhere, traditionally owning a home was thought of as essential, a place to live or perhaps even to work and certainly something to aspire to. Now it has become much more than this. With rising rates, property is now considered to be a solid asset class, something that investment managers recommend adding to your portfolio. If you look closely, you will see that as an investor you have the opportunity to profit from a property purchase as long as you get in at the right time.

Investing in real estate is a good call but it is an expensive and tedious affair, one that will tie up your money for a few years. It is the perfect example of an illiquid investment.

WHAT THE EXPERTS SAY

Is investing in property a good idea? Or is it better to stick with equities?

'Portfolio allocation in India specifically has very few limited lucrative options as against the international scenario. Considering the transparency levels and regulatory environment in India, it is advisable to have diversified asset allocation and not put all your eggs in one basket.

Average annualized return from equities has been one-third of that generated from real estate in the last five years. Going forward, we continue to see robust returns from real estate, but investor expectations have to be toned down as returns that you get today may not be equivalent to the returns investors have made in the last five years.

With a stable government at the centre, we continue to see both asset classes doing well. Fundamentals are currently robust and will further improve in both these asset classes.'

– **Om Ahuja**

CEO, Jones Lang LaSalle India

Mira and Vivek Bhattacharya invested in property back in 1996. '*My husband and I were to keen to purchase a home because we believed that it was the right thing to do for our family. We were living in Mumbai at the time but we couldn't afford anything there. So after attending a property development fair, we decided to put our money into a residential house worth ₹40 lakh in Banarghatta, a suburb of Bangalore. It was an upcoming area with the development of the IT industry. We thought, how can we go wrong?*'

Seven months into their payments of instalments, however, there was still no sign of a title certificate. That's when Mira's husband got suspicious. '*He wanted to stop the payments immediately. It led to a lot of arguments between us because by that time, we had already paid ₹23 lakh – more than half the price of the property. But he didn't want to throw more good money after bad.*'

Unfortunately for the Bhattacharyas, that was ₹23 lakhs of their hard-earned money down the drain. For the longest time, they simply ignored the situation but then, a couple of years later, a relative urged them to take the developer to court. By the time the Bhattacharyas got around to filing a suit against the developer, he had absconded with the cash and was nowhere to be found. Whether it was a scam deal or just a deal gone wrong, the bottom line was that the Bhattacharyas never saw that money again.

Such situations have become commonplace in India. With rapid development taking place, many people have given up their professions to become property developers as it is a good business to be in these days, but this also means that it has become increasingly difficult to find a reliable developer whom you can trust with your money.

What about property bubbles? How do you protect yourself from them?

Well, on one hand, you have to understand that there is some risk associated with all kinds of investment. That said, Rajesh Krishnan believes that the risks associated with property are not related to market movements.

'I wouldn't be concerned about prices crashing as demand is always more than supply,' says Rajesh. *'The risks are conditional, they lie not in the prices of property itself but in things like taking credit exposure on the developer, due diligence on land and title and so forth.'*

He points out that, *'Affordable homes are built using customer money and the developers are not necessarily always creditworthy. The important thing is that you have to buy from someone you trust – preferably from a big brand.'*

Investing in property: down to the brass tacks

The first thing you have to ask yourself is what kind of property you are looking to invest in. Is it a home, an office, or something else to build your investment portfolio?

Needless to say, there is a huge difference between the three. Until recently, buying a home in India was considered a sentimental decision. But soaring prices in recent years have made our growing middle class turn to real estate as a means of generating wealth.

You should understand that buying a home to live in is not strictly an investment. Sure, it is an asset which can be used or leveraged if necessary, but a home that you live in will not give you returns. So once you have a home of your own, it's a good idea to look at another property purely for investment purposes – one that fetches you returns through rent and appreciation, among other things.

When you go to buy property for your personal use, for example, your first apartment or flat, you make that decision keeping in mind your particular wants and needs. However, when you buy property as an investment you need to think differently.

When you are buying a home in which you will live, you

might want to invest in a certain size of apartment to house your family or you might want to purchase your property in a particular town or part of town because your friends or family live close by. You might want to put in more money on a new building with amenities like a gym or because it is located close to where you work.

None of this really matters if you are buying a flat or an office that you plan to rent out. As a landlord your position is totally different. You will look at spending as little as possible and yet being able to rent it out for as much as possible.

Ten things to consider when you add property investment to your portfolio.

- What is the ideal property size for you?
- In which part of town should you purchase it?
- Are you going to live in it, or do you plan to rent it out?
- How close is it to schools, colleges, hospitals and public transportation?
- Does the building offer the following amenities? Security systems, waste-disposal services, road cleaning, pest control, parking spaces, water and power supply
- What kind of value-added amenities – for example, a garden, gym, children's play area, clubhouse – does the building offer?
- What is the re-sale potential of the property?
- What is your rental yield?
- How much can you expect the property to appreciate in value?
- Will it give you stable returns in the long term?

So what all must you ensure before embarking on acquiring property? Here are some points:

Have a reliable source of income

Buying property is a long-term commitment. It requires significant funding and is an investment that you need to think about staying in for at least five to seven years. This is very different from investing in stocks or bonds, which you can easily liquify if you need cash.

Property is not cheap, though there are variations depending on which city you live in, or which part of a city you live in. All the major Indian cities have seen double-digit growth in property prices in the last several years. Mumbai is now one of the most expensive cities in the world to buy any kind of property – both commercial and residential – in[5] and with 2,00,000 newcomers each year, Delhi is rapidly rising to join its ranks.[6] Just to get your foot in the door, you would need to pay anywhere between 15 and 25% of the property value as a down payment. Then you need to consider acquisition costs like stamp duties, legal fees, brokerage fees. Once you are done with the down payment, you need to think about monthly payments for the home, insurance costs, taxes and maintenance.

So it is highly likely that you might be looking at putting in the bulk of your savings when you're purchasing property.

Calculate your expenditure according to your income

It's difficult to say how much of your monthly income you should keep aside for property expenses. Remember, these are illiquid investments that you need to hold on to for a longer period of time. Therefore, always plan accordingly. Even if you apply for a home loan, your monthly income is a factor that is taken into account.

Om Ahuja highlights that, '*The home loan lender looks at the annual salary and stability of the borrower in terms of employment.*

The basic criteria also revolves around the borrower's capability to return the loan over the duration for which it is being availed. Normally, the lender looks at lending an amount that can ensure the loan is repaid over a period of 15 to 20 years along with interest.'

Determine the size of the property

It's always tempting to think of the biggest as best but that may not be practical. Ask yourself the crucial questions. Are you buying your first home as a single person, or with your partner? If so, you are not likely to need too much space – but then you might want to start a family in the near future. If you are upgrading to a second home, see what the situation is. Have your kids have grown up and gone away, or has your family grown so much that you need more space? Your unique situation will affect your property purchase.

If you are buying property only from the investment point of view, you could think about buying a small apartment in a good area, as it will be easy to rent out.

Consider the resale value

Even if you are emotionally attached to your property, you must think about it from the point of view of a seller because only then can you begin to understand its true value. This is difficult for many of us, especially if we are first-time homeowners, but as nuclear families invariably expand into subsequent generations it is likely that more people will sell their properties. So when you purchase a property, regardless of whether it is your home or your office or something that you will rent out for years before selling it, you must think about the person who will buy it, that is, the person you eventually sell it to, and what will make her want to buy it from you.

What is the USP of your property?

Does it have a nice view? Is it conveniently located near restaurants and shopping malls? Is it in a quiet part of town where you can escape the humdrum of the city? Does the building offer value-added services like gyms, gardens or a clubhouse?

Make sure the property is reasonably priced

You can do this by walking in the neighbourhood and researching the market value of the neighbouring buildings. Find out if any of the surrounding properties are for sale. If so, what are they priced at? There are several online brokers such as Magic Bricks and 99acres who compare the values of properties in a specific area of town.

You can also look at the National Housing Bank's (NHB) Residex which is an index for tracking residential real estate in India.

NHB Residex
Base Year: 2007 = 100

Delhi NCR | Bengaluru | Mumbai | Kolkata | Bhopal | Hyderabad | Faridabad | Patna | Ahmedabad | Chennai | Jaipur | Lucknow | Pune | Surat | Kochi | Bhubaneshwar | Guwahati | Ludhiana | Vijayawada | Indore | Chandigarh | Coimbatore | Dehradun | Meerut | Nagpur | Raipur

CITY WISE HOUSING PRICE INDEX FOR THE QUARTER APRIL–JUNE, 2014

Cities	2007 Index	Apr-Jun 2012 Index	Jul-Sep 2012 Index	Oct-Dec 2012 Index	Jan-Mar 2013 Index	Apr-Jun 2013 Index	Jul-Sep 2013 Index	Oct-Dec 2013 Index	Jan-March 2014 Index	Apr-June 2014 Index
Hyderabad	100	85	84	90	88	84	88	93	95	95
Faridabad	100	217	216	205	207	202	204	209	209	211
Patna	100	140	138	151	152	147	150	159	150	154
Ahmedabad	100	174	180	191	192	186	191	197	209	213
Chennai	100	309	312	314	310	303	318	330	349	355
Jaipur	100	78	85	87	112	110	108	105	101	102
Lucknow	100	171	175	189	183	187	191	185	194	193
Pune	100	200	201	205	221	219	219	235	232	241

Surat	100	145	138	150	140	142	145	154	165	161
Kochi	100	73	80	87	89	86	86	85	85	86
Bhopal	100	207	206	216	230	227	220	223	226	229
Kolkata	100	196	191	209	197	189	199	196	206	211
Mumbai	100	197	196	217	222	221	222	222	229	233
Bengaluru	100	100	98	106	109	108	107	111	107	108
Delhi NCR	100	172	178	195	202	199	190	195	199	193
Bhubaneshwar	100	164	168	172	197	195	193	202	195	196
Guwahati	100	159	158	166	153	147	149	160	154	159
Ludhiana	100	171	168	179	167	157	150	150	145	147

Updated every quarter, it covers all the major cities and the sub-areas in them, comparing them to the base index (the year of 2007, valued at 100) as well as to the previous quarter. The index value will tell you how real estate prices are doing in a particular area or city. Here's an example of a Residex from the National Housing Board.

You can see that aside from Hyderabad and Kochi, home prices in all Indian cities have risen since the base year of 2007. What you are looking to do is to make sure that you are not putting your money into a property that is overpriced compared to others in the neighbourhood.

Ascertain your returns

One way to ensure that the property is not overpriced is to think about the ***rental yield*** – in other words, how much you can rent it out for. It's a good idea to do this even if you are not planning to rent it out because it will give you a fair estimate of the worth of your investment – rental field essentially measures the returns you can get on your property without considering the expected capital gain or loss. Rental field is calculated by dividing your expected annual rent by your purchase price. For example, if you earn an annual rent of ₹1 lakh on a property which is priced at ₹50 lakh, then the rental yield is 2%.

You can also buy property for commercial reasons. Om Ahuja says commercial rental yields in the major Indian cities range from anywhere from 7% to 10%. Jones Lang LaSalle, a property research firm tells us that Grade A office and retail rents are rising in all major Indian cities – Mumbai, Delhi, Bangalore, Chennai. So if you are looking to add property investment to your portfolio, you might want to consider investing in commercial property in one of these markets so that you can maximize your returns by benefiting from both rental yield and capital appreciation.[7]

Having said that, we want to caution you that rental yields work differently for residential and commercial properties in different parts of the country and the world. The reality is that, currently, India has some of the lowest rental yields in the world – about 2% to 5% overall. The rental yields in Delhi are around 2%, in Noida they are 3%, while Mumbai and Gurgaon fare only slightly better at 3.5%. Hyderabad, Kolkata and Bangalore all fall within the 3–4% range and Pune quotes a rental yield of up to 2–3%. For other smaller cities, rental markets are not developed or uniform. This is about 30–40% of what you can get by investing in a bank fixed deposit. Doesn't sound too promising, does it?

But before you strike this one off your list, you need to be aware that investing in property is not just about what you can get in rent. There is also the consideration of what you can get on pure capital appreciation. Om Ahuja points out that if you consider only this factor you'll find that you are getting 6–10% annual returns for commercial property and 10–15% annual returns for residential property. This puts a whole new light on the property investment story.

This is a problem which you will find in emerging markets all over the world. Even though you don't get much rent for the properties, the capital appreciation is huge because the countries are developing and foreign investors want to come in and take advantage of low prices today for higher returns tomorrow. Since India is still an emerging economy, as an investor you have the opportunity to pump funds into the real estate sector for high returns from capital appreciation.[8]

WHAT THE EXPERTS SAY

Why should you focus on rental yield versus capital appreciation?

'Commercial property is primarily bought from the rental yield aspect and residential is bought from the capital appreciation aspect. The investment budget for a commercial property should be anywhere upwards of US $1 million whereas a budget for residential properties can be as little as US $500 and upwards from there. Considering the commercial format and the investor's budget, it is their call to buy an office format or retail outlet.'

– **Om Ahuja**
CEO, Jones Lang La Salle, India

Don't feel awkward about negotiating

Too many women investors are concerned about losing a property investment opportunity because they are concerned that by bargaining they might offend the seller. Not at all! It's worth remembering that buying property is no different from walking down Zaveri Bazaar to bargain for a piece of gold jewellery.

Make sure that you are not in a hurry and that you take the time to consider the property and all the ancillary factors, and then offer what you think is the fair price, regardless of what the landlord has listed the property for. If you are going to allocate a significant portion of your savings, it is important that you should feel comfortable about your investment.

WHAT THE EXPERTS SAY

Is it better for the Indian woman to invest in commercial property or residential property?

'For individual investors, buying the right property is crucial. One needs to look at growth potential, ease of leasing, whether it is exit-friendly and, most importantly, her budget. Investing in commercial property requires a different mind-set from investing in a residential one. The two have different challenges and growth characteristics. If the budget is limited, buying a small commercial property will always pose challenges for the investor: the parties that the investor will have to deal with for leasing will be small; and the investor will also face challenges in making tenants exit. Investors in larger commercial (office/shops) formats normally deal with large reputed players and the risks are lower. But here investors need larger budgets and bandwidth to find the right tenant at the right time.

Returns from residential asset-leasing may not be exciting but it's easy to find tenants and the real upside is the capital appreciation. Considering growing urbanization and nuclear family formats, we continue to see demand picking up in cities with good employment opportunities.'

– **Om Ahuja**

CEO, Jones Lang LaSalle India

What are property funds?

Property funds are essentially mutual funds that provide an opportunity to diversify your portfolio in property, which is regarded as an alternative investment. If you do not have the funds to invest in property but would like to expose your portfolio to the Indian property sector then one way to go is to buy into a property fund. Until recently, this was impossible to do as a retail investor, because property funds were only available to large private equity investors who could have a stake in the company in return for injecting a huge amount of cash into it. Even now, most property mutual funds require significantly large investment so they are in essence more suited to the high net-worth investor rather than the middle-class investor.

Aside from this, they are plagued by a whole set of problems. These funds are not transparent and are relatively illiquid. You don't have visibility as to where your money is tied up, the process of buying and selling the underlying assets is very complicated, and the complex legal framework just does not support the retail investor.

Amit Jeffrey, Fund Manager of Alternative Assets, Client Associates, explains this: 'When it comes to property funds, the ticket sizes are huge and for investors to get good returns over a three-year period you need a very robust market. You need buyers who are willing to shell out ₹50 to ₹60 crore, to buy an asset that was worth ₹10 crore five years ago. We just don't have that kind of liquidity in the Indian market yet. If you bought an apartment for ₹50 or ₹60 lakh, it's relatively much easier to sell it at a crore a couple of years later.'

Investing in property funds is more suitable for a high net-worth individual as it requires a large amount of funding.

The only benefit in investing in such a fund is that you are not responsible for the maintenance and upkeep of the property since you haven't bought it directly.

Your Money Mantra

Investment in property is a strategy that every smart investor should adopt. Though it sounds intimidating, it can be quite simple. All it requires is due diligence on the investor's part.

- If your budget allows it, consider investing in property sooner rather than later so that you can ride the wave of urban development.
- Consider your objectives when you decide to put your money in property, whether it is a residential property, a commercial one or a property fund.
- If you are buying property for investment purposes, consider its resale value. Put in your money only after you are satisfied with the estimated rental yield and capital appreciation.
- Always buy through trusted sources.

STEP 4

Investing in art

ABOUT FOUR YEARS AGO, ROHINA MALKANI WAS KEEN TO INVEST a portion of her portfolio in alternative assets but she wasn't keen on the idea of property as she owned her home jointly with her husband. She had already invested in gold, and other options like long-short funds and commodities just didn't appeal to her. More than anything, she wanted to buy art because she loved art – but she was too conservative to spend so much money for the sake of her love for art.

'*If I was going to put my money in an expensive piece of art, then I needed to be convinced that it would get me some rate of return*,' says Rohina. '*So I investigated with art houses like Saffronart in Mumbai and Delhi, and also directly with the artists who were showing their works at different galleries. They offered beautiful pieces and the likelihood of this and that but nobody was willing to guarantee anything. I couldn't risk putting money down, for example, on a Jayasri Burman piece that I loved because who knows where or how I'd be able to sell it, and when? And when it came to emerging artists like Dilip*

Kale or Archana Gupta, nobody was willing to talk about anything beyond the aesthetics of the painting.'

Somewhat disillusioned, Rohina had almost given up on the idea when a friend based in Hong Kong suggested that she look at purchasing a work by a European master from Collins & Kent International Dealers. She herself had purchased a Picasso from them a few years earlier and had already made money on capital appreciation and rent by leasing it to a company through the art dealer's rental programme.

At first, Rohina was hesitant. '*I thought, how could I possibly afford a European master? But when I found out that my friend had specifically chosen a Picasso lithograph for less than US $5,000, I thought maybe this is something I can invest in as well.*'

It took some time and due diligence, but by December 2013 Rohina had decided to purchase a unique red and gold butterfly from Damien Hirst's 'Souls' collection. It cost her US $6,000, about ₹3.5 lakh. '*I specifically chose these colours because the Chinese consider them auspicious. I planned to buy this in Hong Kong, rent it out in Hong Kong with the idea of eventually selling it to a buyer in Hong Kong. My buyer would naturally be Chinese so I planned for that from the beginning.*'

In February 2014, her client services associate at Collins & Kent sent Rohina a note to wish her a happy new year and to let her know that the value of her Damien Hirst had gone up by US $2,200. You can imagine Rohina's delight at the situation.

'*Ever since then, I've been on cloud nine!*' she says. '*I would like to save more with my equity investments to hopefully add to my art portfolio in a few years.*'

The world outside India considers fine art to be a highly

sought-after asset – not just for aesthetics or historical importance, but also because it is a genuine and dependable investment. Even though Indian investors struggle with the idea today, it is just a matter of time before things change. In fact, initial steps towards such a change have already begun, as is proved by the fact that much of the money going into art investment today comes from buyers in the BRIC countries, including India.

What's great about investing in art is that it offers long-term security, documented growth, and reliability during uncertain economic conditions. Couple this with ground-breaking rental potential, something that the Canadians had discovered long ago in the '70s and the Australians in the '80s, and you have a winner!

How to choose what kind of art to invest in

Of course, not every piece of art is going to provide capital growth or yield returns.

You have to be very circumspect about what you buy and what you do with it. According to Michael Donnan, the Asia Pacific Art Director of Collins & Kent International Art Dealers, you should buy a piece which has good potential for medium- to long-term growth, and then rent it out to a third party to generate a significant rental income in the short term.

'*Rental yields alone can average 7.5% per annum of the value of the work being rented out, and rental contract durations across the industry are typically one and two years*,' says Donnan.

Not bad, isn't it? But how do you find a work of art that has potential?

Art dealers across the globe agree that by far the international art market continues to be dominated by Western art and artists like Andy Warhol, Pablo Picasso and Gerhard Richter.

On one level, this is very unfortunate because as an Indian investor you might want to invest in a painting by M.F. Hussain or Anjolie Ela Menon or an emerging Indian artist like Rajib Surroy. However, art advisors across the globe affirm that this strategy is not ideal for investment purposes.

'*If you are buying art for the love of it, that's a different story, but if you are buying art as an investment then you need to think about your future buyer*,' says Michael Donnan. '*Sure, there are markets for different kinds of art but those markets are usually limited to the genre of the artist. South Asians are indeed the predominant buyers of South Asian art, as are the Chinese for Chinese heritage and contemporary art, or Australians for Aboriginal art*.'

The size of the Indian art market (quoted to be around US $100 million) is not tiny by any means but it is nothing compared to Western markets where just one painting can sell for more than that amount. The local art market, in fact, grew frenetically between 2000 and 2008, but there has been a long slump since then.

Art Tactic, which is a go-to guide for art investors around the world, said that confidence levels in the Indian art market fell significantly in 2013 because of the fall of the rupee.

But not everyone agrees with this.

'*The Indian art market does appear undervalued*,' says Dinesh Vazirani, the founder of Saffronart, '*hence in the long term, I believe it is a good investment. China accounted for 24% of the global art market in 2013 while India comprised less than 1%, despite China's GDP being only 3.5 times more than India's. Surely such a gap cannot sustain over the long term. Indian collectors will also participate in greater numbers in my opinion, emulating the rise of the Chinese art market*.'

But purchasing European masters is another story as they have universal appeal simply because of their brand value. There will always be a market for a Chagall or a Matisse, so the value is always going to increase. The same goes for Picasso. Rohina's friend in Hong Kong doesn't even like Picasso as an artist but when it comes to re-sale she knows that putting her dollars into a Picasso lithograph is her best bet.

There is a whole range of artists you can invest in. Deceased and non-producing like Picasso, Rembrandt and Matisse; blue-chip and living ones like Damien Hirst and Andy Warhol; and career artists and emerging artists like Banksy.

There is also hierarchy in the value of artworks based on their medium. Generally sculpture is the most expensive, followed by paintings, then water colours, and works on paper, which can be quite reasonable. This really brings the investment grade art within the reach of the amateur female investor.

'*Works on paper are certainly more affordable than oil paintings. Works by emerging and mid-career artists start as low as US $500 and those by deceased and non-producing artists like Picasso begin at US $5,000,*' says Michael Donnan.

And if that's not enough then get this – just as there are indices to track assets classes like equity, debt and emerging markets, the Mindshare art index tracks the leading artists of all time.

What makes the whole thing really tick for an investor like Rohina is the fact that once you have bought the art, you can directly place it in a rental programme where the gallery owner rents it out at a rate of 7.5% or so for the minimum duration of one year. Not a bad way to recoup your investment and gain capital appreciation, right?

KEY POINTS TO REMEMBER

As with any investment, there are a few essential questions you must have clear answers to before investing in works on paper.

- **How well-known is the artist?**[9]

  Artists who have achieved global recognition (especially deceased or non-producing artists) offer the investor a far larger rental and resale market than artists who have smaller audiences or cult followings.

- **Is the artwork in good condition?**

  A work in good condition has a much higher resale value. Works on paper that are framed according to conservation standards are able to maintain their condition and avoid decay and damage over time.

- **Provenance and authenticity**

  Works accompanied by good provenance and proof of authenticity offer greater resale opportunities.

- **Is there a documented history of price growth available?**

  A number of publications such as the Printworld Directory detail the growth in value of rare and sold-out editions from the date of their creation to their present-day recommended retail values.

- **Rarity**

  The artwork may have specific unique annotations or dedications not found in the commercial edition. It may also be a proof produced during a conceptual or creative process, meaning that it has significant historic importance and is therefore of considerably higher value to collectors.

The idea of investing in art might not seem like rocket science, at least not compared to investing in equities and fixed income, but we must add a word of caution here. Although art can be a great asset, do not think for a moment that investing in it doesn't carry any associated risks. It's much easier for less seasoned investors to rely on higher returns from building a portfolio of securities because – let's face it – not all of us are blessed with the ability to select a winning piece of art. Of course, there is nothing to stop you from sharpening your art investing skills over time. It's all about understanding the science behind how to select art as an investment opportunity rather than purely for love and aesthetics

SHOPPERS GUIDE FOR BUYING ART

Dinesh Vazirani, Founder and CEO, Saffronart

Art sales can be done through auction houses, galleries or private dealers. Whereas auction houses will sell through auctions or privately, galleries and dealers will re-sell works only privately. Galleries will also re-sell works through public or private exhibitions. All three act as intermediaries and handle everything from selling to shipping the works to the clients. There are pros and cons to approaching an auction house versus approaching private dealers or galleries.

Let's look at these factors from both a buyer's and a seller's perspective.

Price

Prices are fixed at private sales though there may be some negotiation between buyer and seller. At auctions, you could see your artwork go for stratospheric prices while or, on the other hand, buyers can get bargains below their estimated value. If you approach an auction house, you will be asked to specify a minimum price – the reserve price – and if that price is not reached, the artwork will be returned to you.

In the case of private sales, your work will be sold for the mutually agreed price, which may be below its true market potential. In terms of investment, one can say auctions entail more risk for the seller with a greater potential for reward, whereas private sales mitigate the risk and the reward.

For the buyer, auctions can be an opportunity to obtain works at low value, but prices may also end up getting out of reach. For an auction sale, both buyers and sellers pay a percentage to the auction house. The 'Buyer's Premium' paid by the buyer is based on a published tiered structure with the percentage decreasing at higher values. The seller's commission is negotiated between the auction house and the seller and is generally lower for higher value artworks. In the case of a private sale, the dealer's commission is usually charged only to the seller and built into the agreed price.

Anonymity and access

Both auctions and private sales, when transacted through credible intermediaries (auction houses, galleries, dealers), provide anonymity to the seller and the buyer. However, the auction catalogue for a given auction is distributed widely and available on auction house websites, which is not the case for private sales.

This exposure benefits the seller as it reaches a larger number of buyers, but it also means that if the owner of an artwork is well known then people in the art fraternity will know who the seller is. The open nature of auctions means that any buyer with a good credit history can register to bid in an auction, whereas private sales by their very nature are restricted to a smaller group known to the dealer.

Since it is publicly known when a work does not sell in auction, it is advisable that you don't put it up for auction again for some period of time as there is a risk of over-exposing it, whereas private sales do not carry this risk.

Choices and competition

When you put up a work on auction, that work will feature with, say, 100 to 300 or so other lots. While that range of choice is a great advantage for buyers, and from a seller's perspective attracts a larger number of buyers, it can also work against the seller as their work is competing against others in the catalogue.

For a seller, it is advisable to ask the auction house if it is featuring similar works from the same artist to get a sense for what the work might be competing with.

Your Money Mantra

An art piece is not only a great aesthetic addition to your personal collection but can also double up as a source of income. Compared to an option like property, it requires far less maintenance.

- When you buy a piece of art from an investment point-of-view, go back to the old Warren Buffet philosophy and think about whether there will be a market for it when you want to sell it.
- It will work to your advantage if you invest in a work by an international master. But if you want to buy from a local artist, keep the prospective buyer in mind before taking a decision.

Your Money, Our Expert Plan

By now you have accumulated a whole lot of information about various asset classes and how to build your portfolio, but you might still be wondering where to begin and how. Don't worry! We've put together some recommendations to help you assimilate the information so that you can get going. Always remember our eternal mantra – it is not rocket science. If we could do it, chances are that you can do it much better!

For your younger years

This is the stage in your life when you need to accumulate wealth. You might be young and unmarried, or you might be married with young children. You might be working and earning or you might have given up work to look after your children. Any way you look at it, you need to save your money and accumulate your wealth for the long term (your long-term goal is always retirement).

Here's what you ideally need to do:

- Invest the larger part of your portfolio in equities.
- Choose a low-cost term-insurance policy.
- Consider an equity-linked savings scheme for tax benefits.

- Invest in property. This will be a very good asset and will give great returns in the future.

For your middle years

At this stage in your life you may have cleared off large debts like home and education loans but you still have maintenance expenses, and maybe even wedding expenses for your children.

This is usually a transition stage where some of your financial goals are yet to be achieved. Although you still might have a regular source of income, there is a chance that you might have to dip into your savings to fulfil these new goals and responsibilities.

Here's what you ideally need to do:

- At this stage, you should have a balanced portfolio with equal portions dedicated to equities and debt instruments.

For your senior years

Your income is at its highest just before your retirement and it declines substantially post retirement. You might have huge medical bills and maintain a certain standard of life without a regular source of income. Now the time has come to reap the benefits of your investments.

Here's what you ideally need to do:

- Invest in debt securities, but be sure that you understand these completely – aside from fixed deposits, there are very few pure debt securities out there.
- A number of schemes are announced from time to time to help senior citizens save tax and also earn better returns. For example, in case of bank FDs, senior citizens typically get a higher rate of interest (between 0.5–1%) than others.

For unmarried working women

If you are unmarried and are undertaking higher studies, or working full-time or doing both on a part-time basis, then you are at that very particular juncture in your life when you have all the freedom to try new things, take risks and go the extra-mile. This is the best period when you should ideally start investing. This phase would act as the foundation for your future investments.

Here's what you ideally need to do:

- For your short-term investment options, you could choose from hybrid bank accounts, bank FDs, Post Office deposits and liquid mutual funds.
- For your long-term investment option, you can choose an equity-based mutual fund. Try to choose a midcap equity fund for a period of 5 years or more. Or you can invest in stocks separately.
- Gold bullions are also a good option for you.
- Last, but certainly the most important option, is buying property.

For married working women

If you are married and working, you may be juggling home and a job or a business, and might lack sufficient time to make informed financial decisions and to track your investments regularly. So the best investments for you may be those that have minimum limited risk and those that do not need constant attention. You could also take assistance from a good financial planner.

Here's what you need to do:

- You can invest your money in CFDs, PPF and bank FDs for the short term.
- For the long term, you can invest in property and debt instruments like bonds.
- Since you have a regular source of income you can afford to be a bit aggressive in your investment strategy. Invest in stocks and be prepared to stay in for a longer period.
- Mutual funds having both debt and equity components as well as liquid funds are also a great alternative to build your portfolio.
- Buy property. If you already have a primary residential property, consider buying another (residential or commercial) property just for investment purposes.

For homemakers

If you are a homemaker and do not have any personal source of income, you may want to invest the savings you make every month by efficiently managing your family's budget.

You not only want to make every penny count but to make sure every penny grows. Get your money to work for you rather than keeping it idle in your cupboard safe. Invest your savings in hybrid bank accounts which earn higher interest vis-à-vis normal bank accounts.

Here's what you ideally need to do:

- Since you work on a tight budget, monthly savings are your best strategy. Invest in an RD in a bank or at the post office.
- Invest in gold mutual funds or buy gold in electronic form. This will save you the depreciation cost due to wear and tear.
- Liquid funds are also a great option for you as they will ensure easy availability of cash and also preserve your money.

For single women

(With or without dependants)

If you are a single woman or a single parent, you might bear the responsibility of providing for yourself and your children. You should look for investments that do not leave any of your goals to chance. Above all, review your investment portfolio every month to weed out anything that could possibly pose a risk to your financial goals.

Here's what you need to do:

- Invest in a liquid fund or hybrid savings account.
- Buy a term-insurance plan to provide your family with an economic buffer from misfortunes in your absence.
- Buy gold in bullion form or invest in property for the long term.

Globalizing your portfolio

WHY STAY LOCAL WHEN YOU CAN GO GLOBAL?

'Not only does a global perspective provide insight into alternative investment opportunities outside the domestic market, but it also offers much-needed diversification benefits for your portfolio.'

– **Deborah Yang**
Managing Director and Head of the MSCI Index, EMEA

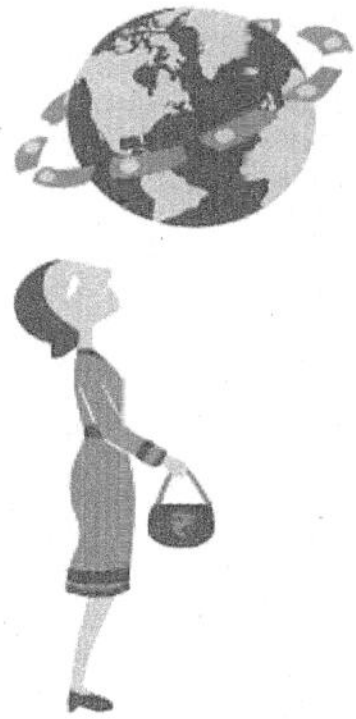

STEP 1

Going global

NOW THAT YOU ARE CLOSE TO BEING AN EXPERT WITH REGARD to investing in India, you are probably wondering whether it's possible to diversify your portfolio by investing abroad. We are here to tell you that it is not only possible for you to do so, but it is also a *must* for any smart investor.

Douglas Clayton, CEO of Leopard Capital, a private equity investment firm, believes that it is imperative for the Indian woman to invest at least some portion of her portfolio abroad because if you invest only in one country (and countries like India specifically), you are exposed to macro-economic risks that are distinct for that one country. '*Diversification requires you to invest a portion of your money outside of your own country and in many different asset classes,*' says Clayton. '*India and other emerging markets tend to be more volatile so it would be good for an Indian woman to get exposure to some of the developed markets which tend to be less volatile. A good, low-cost way for her to do this is through ETFs [Exchange Traded Funds]*.'

There are different ways of exposing your portfolio to foreign markets – through mutual funds, direct investment in equities, ETFs, commodities and even real estate, though buying foreign stocks, mutual funds and ETFs is much easier and more liquid than buying real estate abroad.

Investing abroad is also a good way to secure your money against local geo-political or economic events. Mutual funds are particularly interesting as they offer different avenues if you are looking to invest abroad: you can buy ***international funds*** that invest in foreign stocks, or ***feeder funds*** that direct money into foreign funds, or you can invest in something called a ***fund of funds***, which puts your money in multiple foreign funds. In order to understand how it is done and the repercussions such an investment might have, let's take a look at Sherie's story.

In 2007, Sherie Mazumdar decided to invest some of her money outside India. The country's apex bank, RBI, allowed it, so she thought why not participate in the Internet boom that everyone was talking about.

'*I was dying to globalize my portfolio and since I didn't know how to do it, I actually sent $20,000 to my cousin in the US and asked her to invest on my behalf – some of it in Internet stocks and some in the housing market. I had another cousin in the UK and I asked her to invest my money in UK stocks. The rest of it I invested right here through a feeder fund that fed into the US stock market*,' she recalls.

Despite her good intentions, Sherie's plan backfired completely as her investment was exposed to some of the major financial crises in the West. The USA and the UK both went into recession following the global financial crisis of 2008. '*The value of my investments dropped significantly*,' says Sherie. '*I was miserable during those years. I kept thinking that I could have done much better had I invested in the local market*.'

Is this true? Could Sherie have actually done better by keeping her money in Indian markets?

Well yes, but the situation wouldn't have been as rosy as it looks. It's true that, unlike many other countries, India did not go into recession. Even so, we had to face our own set of problems with markets going through a rough patch after the event. Equity investors took a severe beating as their portfolios yielded less-than-desirable results. It took a few years for the equity markets to get back to pre-2008 levels.

'*See, the equity markets have done well but it has taken time*,' says Devesh Chawla, a portfolio manager formerly with Client Associates. '*In January 2008, the Sensex was at 21,000; in April 2014, it touched the 22,500 mark. No doubt the investors made up for any losses that they had incurred, but those who had joined when the market was at the peak managed to gain only 1,500 points.*'

Sherie's portfolio was affected badly because she had invested her money only in the developed markets abroad. There are positives and negatives attached to this.

Investing abroad gives you the opportunity to hedge your local investments as you are now investing in another currency – most likely US dollars. However, if you are investing in a country which is already at a significant stage of development, then you have less opportunity to participate in their overall economic growth story. The UK, the Eurozone and the US are well developed with urban infrastructure and multinational companies in place. They can definitely get you some returns, but these will probably not be as high as the returns from an economy which has significant growth potential, such as India's.

When it comes to investing in developed countries, many foreign investors prefer a destination like Silicon Valley with its tech companies. This is because if you choose them carefully as soon as they go public, they can potentially offer you higher rate of returns. Investing in leading companies such as Google, Apple or Samsung might give your portfolio the edge that you have been looking for. It's always good to diversify, although experts suggest that you don't invest more than 5–10% of your overall portfolio in foreign stocks.

KEY POINTS TO REMEMBER

- Globalize your investments in order to diversify your portfolio and capture market cycles across the globe.
- Take this step only after your portfolio is well diversified across domestic Indian markets.
- Determine how much the RBI will actually let you invest abroad. The RBI has now limited this to US $250,000 per financial year.
- Invest when the rupee is strong as it will enable you to purchase more abroad.
- Do your research and understand the risks involved. For example, investing in the US market means exposing your investment to micro and macroeconomic situations affecting the US economy. You can also put your money into a fund that invests in multiple countries.

This will reduce your country-specific risk through further diversification.

- Across debt and equity assets, performance tends to be country-specific. Secure your investments by investing in developed markets like the US or Europe that are more consumer-oriented, as well as in developing economies that are driven by inflation and growth.
- Always compare the P/E multiple of the country index in which you are investing against the specific stock or mutual fund you want to invest in.
- Understand that you will be taking a currency risk. So if you invest a lakh in foreign stocks or mutual funds at a time when the dollar is equal to ₹60, your investment will be US $1,666.67. If it grows by 10%, then it becomes worth US $1,833.33 or ₹1.1 lakh. But if the rupee has since then strengthened to, say, ₹55 per US dollar then the currency fluctuation will eat into your returns and you will get less than ₹1.1 lakh if you encash the amount. On the flip side, if the rupee depreciates to, say, ₹65 per dollar, then you will get more for your dollar.
- Look into tax benefit schemes. Many debt-fund tax norms are applicable for global funds even if they have equity exposure. Also, be aware of tax rules that differ from country to country.

Your Money Mantra

While globalizing your portfolio, you need to be aware of the currency risks. Do this when the rupee is strong, as that will enable you to purchase more abroad.

- It might be a good strategy to invest in developing economies rather than in developed ones as the former offer more scope for growth.
- The downside of investing in an emerging economy is increased volatility. A developed market, on the other hand, offers more consistent returns minus the risk.

STEP 2

Exploring emerging economies

AS WE MENTIONED AT THE OUTSET, INVESTING IN DEVELOPED markets does not necessarily give you the maximum growth potential for your rupee, or should we say dollar? Let's stretch this beyond dollars to other currencies as well, because the markets which have further scope for development may offer investments denominated in currencies besides the US dollar. This is evident in the case of emerging markets and frontier markets.

Emerging Markets

An ***emerging market*** is a country that has some characteristics of a developed market like the US or UK but, in fact, still has a long way to go in terms of development. Typically, this refers to a country in the process of rapid growth and industrialization.[1] This information is relevant for any investor looking to globalize her portfolio, because if you invest early in a country's infrastructural development either directly or through its capital markets, you could get a significantly high return as long as you are willing to stay in for the long run.

India and China are considered to be the two largest emerging economies but the ASEAN–China Free Trade Area is the largest regional emerging market in the world. Some analysts also consider Iran an emerging market.[2]

By investing in Indian assets, you are essentially investing in one of the largest emerging markets in the world by default, but you might want to look outside of the country and invest in other emerging markets. There can be many reasons for doing this. '*You might have a situation where all the emerging markets are doing well and India is not*,' says Douglas Clayton, '*maybe because it is mismanaging its macroeconomic policy or it is not at the right point in its economic cycle. Just because it's an emerging market doesn't mean it's interlinked with all other emerging markets. So there are more opportunities out there.*'

Let's look at the other emerging markets and the corresponding investment options available to you.

BRIC, MIKT and BIITS: The emerging economies

BRIC

While the idea of investing in emerging markets might be attractive, there is a wide range of options to choose from. How does one decide? One way is to understand the groups of emerging markets that have been designated by various economists, the oldest of these being the BRIC nations.

The term BRIC is an acronym referring to the four largest

emerging economies according to their Gross Domestic Product (GDP): Brazil, Russia, India and China, which are all supposed to be at similar stages of economic development.[3] The acronym has now become a part of mainstream vocabulary as the world's economic power has shifted from the G7 developed economies towards the developing world.

Coined by Goldman Sachs economist Jim O'Neill in a 2001 paper entitled 'Building Better Global Economic BRICs', the acronym referred to a group of economies that O'Neill suggested could be among the four most dominant economies by the year 2050.[4] A follow-up report released by Goldman Sachs in 2004 stated a massive increase in the size of the middle class in BRIC nations, indicating a steep rise in demand for not just the basic goods but higher-priced commodities as well.

So what does this mean for India?

If you read the research carefully, you will see the wisdom in increasing your exposure to debt and equity markets, specifically in the manufacturing sector. According to their research, demand for consumer and higher priced goods will grow. By this logic, putting your money in companies that manufacture such goods can only be a good thing for your investment portfolio.

A follow-up report released in 2007 refers to the rapid growth of three sectors that could potentially bring high returns for your investment. It states that: '*India has 10 of the 30 fastest-growing urban areas in the world and, based on current trends, we estimate a massive 700 million people will move to cities by 2050. This will have significant implications for demand of urban infrastructure, real estate and services*.'[5]

The growth opportunity in real estate is particularly interesting, as housing will always top the list of basic human rights and needs. We've already talked about investment opportunities in real estate extensively but, increasingly, there is an indication that as countries like India urbanize, the demand for affordable housing will outstrip the supply.

According to Sachin Sandhir, Managing Director, Royal Institution of Chartered Surveyors (RICS) South Asia, *'Non-availability of affordable housing is as much a problem of the middle-income groups as it is of the lower income groups. In their ability to find appropriate abode, many across mid-income and lower income groups opt for sub-standard housing in the informal sector.'*[6]

But it's important to remember that this applies to other BRIC countries, too.

WHAT THE EXPERTS SAY

How do you decide which emerging market to buy into?

'There are essentially two things you would look at – growth and value. You might decide to invest in Russia because it is cheaper than India. Eventually, there will be a reversion to the mean, so if you hold on long enough, India will follow and Russia will catch up. You can also compare the P/E multiples of different countries. You might use P/Es to determine that you want to put your money in Thailand and China because these have the cheapest markets relative to other countries.'

– **Douglas Clayton**
CEO, Leopard Capital

BIITS

An International Monetary Fund (IMF) background paper prepared for the recent G20 summit talks of a new grouping of vulnerable economies with large current account deficits (CADs). These are Brazil, India, Indonesia, Turkey and South Africa, or BIITS. This new group includes the three BRIC members which have CADs, while excluding the two – China and Russia – which have current account surpluses.[7] An over-dependence on foreign investment to fuel economic growth has caused some turmoil in the BIITS markets. These countries suffer from high levels of inflation, trade deficits and capital flight leading to an overvalued national currency. This is why in 2013 Morgan Stanley created a new expression for these economies – The Fragile Five.

Of course, it's important to remember that economic situations are dynamic. Just a year after the term was coined, the markets of these five countries provided excellent returns.

MINT

The next four largest emerging markets are MINT – Mexico, Indonesia, Nigeria and Turkey.

The term MINT was originally coined by Fidelity Investments, an investment management firm in Boston, but was popularized by Jim O'Neill of Goldman Sachs who considers this group of countries to be the next economic powerhouses. It's a popular and frequently-used term, especially in the investment sector, where it refers to the bonds issued by governments of these countries.[8]

How do you invest in emerging markets?

Let's take a look at two different emerging markets schemes. Both are funds and equity-oriented schemes.

Emerging Markets Fund: The investment objectives, as stated in their fund fact sheet[9] is[10] to provide long-term capital appreciation by investing in India and in the emerging markets, in equity and equity-related instruments, share classes and units or securities issued by overseas mutual funds or unit trusts. The fund may also invest a limited portion in debt and money market instruments.

Global Emerging Markets Fund: The investment objective of the scheme is to provide long-term capital appreciation by investing in an overseas mutual fund scheme that invests in a diversified portfolio of securities as prescribed by SEBI in global emerging markets.

	Minimum Investment	Additional Investment	Top Holding	Benchmark	5-year Return
Emerging Markets Fund	₹1,000	₹1,000	GIF Emerging Markets Equity Fund 99%	MSCI Emerging Market Index	10.20%
Global Emerging Markets Fund	₹5,000	₹1,000	MGF Asian Small Equity Fund Class I 51.93% ishares MSCI Emerging Markets ETF 38.46% T Rowe Price Funds SICAV – Global Emerging Markets Equity Fund 9.04% T Rowe Global Emerging Markets Equity Class A USD 9.04%	MSCI Emerging Market Index	17.75%

Essentially, both funds aim to provide long-term capital appreciation by investing in emerging markets and given below is a snapshot of how these funds operate.

The Emerging Markets Fund is an open-ended fund, meaning

it can issue or redeem shares at any time. Its main holdings, at the time of this particular snapshot, include another Global Emerging Markets Fund.

The Global Emerging Markets Fund is a closed-ended fund, which means that it has already issued all its shares but you can trade shares with other investors. This particular fund shows investments in other funds such as iShares MSCI ETF, Asian Small Equity Funds and other international Emerging Markets Funds.

At the time this particular snapshot was taken, the Global Emerging Markets Fund had a significantly higher 5-year return of 17.75% compared to the Emerging Markets Fund's return of 10.2%. However, this scenario could look different depending on whether they have invested or divested holdings. One problem with both of these funds is that they are not rated by CRISIL.

You can also discuss this with the fund manager of the particular fund, whose contact details will be listed in the fund fact sheet, as this is the person who is actually responsible for investing in the fund's assets.

Frontier Markets

Just like BRIC, MINT and BIITS, ***frontier markets*** are another subset of emerging markets. The term describes the smallest and least developed nations among the emerging markets. The *Wall Street Journal* has described them as 'less liquid, small emerging markets'. Examples of frontier markets include Bhutan, Bulgaria, Croatia, Kazakhstan, Nigeria, Sri Lanka and Vietnam.

Countries on the frontier of growth imply that over time their markets will become more liquid and have similar risk and return characteristics to the larger, more liquid and developed emerging markets.

Frontier markets are different from emerging markets, as emerging markets have some characteristics of a developed market whereas frontier markets are those economies that are on the verge of development. In other words, these are markets surrounded by economic wilderness with far less stable economies, but with plenty of potential to develop over the long term. The term was coined by International Finance Corporation's (IFC) Farida Khambata in 1992. It is possible that a frontier market could become an emerging market over time. However, it is wrong to blatantly assume this.

Frontier markets have lower market capitalization and liquidity than the more developed emerging markets. They are typically pursued by investors seeking high, long-term returns and less likely to be linked with other markets.[11] '*You could argue that India was a frontier market until it became an emerging market about 15 years ago*,' says Douglas Clayton.

According to Clayton, for asset classes like frontier markets, long-term investors are looking for 25% returns per year after all their expenses have been accounted for. But while that may seem a lot, you have to remember there is no guarantee that it'll happen. There is a chance that you could lose money, too.

'*The one thing you should know is that as an asset class frontier markets are considered to be highly volatile products*,' says Clayton. '*This means that the returns vary a lot. If something is risky, it also comes with a lot of rewards and you could make a ton of money on it, but the ups and downs are greater than the usual scenario and you need to be prepared for that*.'

Though this is not a reason to shy away from frontier markets, it all depends on how well you are doing overall with your portfolio and whether you have the ability to take more risk with some small portion of return for possible high reward. As Clayton puts it, '*If a small portion of your money is invested in frontier markets then perhaps you can ride the upswing or accept a downswing.*'

Many frontier market investors insist that investing in frontier assets would actually diversify and reduce risk, which contradicts the general notion that risk would be added by including these markets. This is because they act independently rather than in tandem with the other economies of the world. A financial crisis in a developed country like Greece or currency fluctuations in an emerging market like India do not slow down the demand for more farm products in a frontier market like Cambodia.

Just like other markets, there are a few indices that track frontier markets. For a current list of countries that Morgan Stanley Capital International (MSCI) defines as frontier markets, please refer to Appendix 3a.

It's interesting to note that different investment advisors will have different definitions of what a frontier market is. So while the MSCI list includes a country like Kuwait, Clayton says there is no way he would consider Kuwait to be a frontier market. '*The MSCI is limited to a subset of frontier markets that have a stock market,*' he says. '*So Bhutan would not be included in there because it doesn't have a stock market. Kuwait does, and it fits their loose criteria. We look at markets on a development basis. Frontier markets are the poorest countries in the world. They are poor because their economies are dysfunctional and there lies the opportunity for growth.*'

How do you invest in frontier markets?

Unfortunately, your choices are very limited here. Private equity is not an option as the ticket price is too high for the amateur Indian investor. Mutual funds are the only way out for now, but here too are there are only a handful.

For example, take the Templeton Frontier Markets Fund, which, according to its fact sheet, '*seeks long-term capital appreciation by investing at least 80% of its net assets in securities of companies located in frontier market countries*,' which it defines as countries '*considered to be a subset of those currently defined as developing by the World Bank, the International Finance Corporation, the United Nations, or the countries' authorities, or countries with a stock market capitalization of less than 3% of the MSCI World Index*.'[12] The countries this fund invests in are in the Middle East, Africa, Europe and Asia.

Compare this to the Sanlam African Frontier Markets Fund, which, according to its fund fact sheet, aims to '*achieve long-term capital growth by investing directly or indirectly in African equities*', which their investment manager has identified as being undervalued and offering above-average growth potential.[13]

Both funds are widely diversified – Templeton across countries and Sanlam across industry sectors in African countries. Both are measured against MSCI indices and both have a minimum investment of US $1,000 and have been averaging about 6% returns over five years. These are examples of frontier markets investment options that you could consider for your budget, as opposed to, say, the HSBC GIF Frontier Fund which has an entry ticket price that is too high for the average Indian investor.

At what point does a frontier market switch over to an 'emerging market' status? This, too, is somewhat subjective. MSCI bumped up the UAE and Qatar from frontier to emerging market status in 2014.

'Basically, this is the kind of thing that happens in the most subtle of ways,' says Douglas Clayton. *'When everyone starts talking about them at cocktail parties, perhaps, once a market has actually been "discovered" and institutional capital starts chasing it, it no longer stays cheap. You have to anticipate where the flows are going to happen and then you try to catch it first.'*

Now let's hope that you are attending the right cocktail party!

Your Money Mantra

Beginners should not think much about investing in emerging markets, or frontier markets for that matter, but they should be aware of what these investments are about and track them. Once you have built up your portfolio and have the scope to take more risk, you can think of dabbling in these asset classes.

- Emerging markets offer you the chance to participate in the growth and development of an underdeveloped market and reap high returns in exchange for it.
- Frontier markets are on the fringes of development and present great opportunities for growth, but the risk factor is high and liquidity is low.
- Frontier market economies don't work in tandem and are less likely to be influenced by one another.

STEP 3

Investing abroad: the essentials

NOW THAT YOU KNOW WHERE YOU CAN INVEST YOUR MONEY outside the country, the question that remains is how to do it. One way to do this is through mutual funds. We've already talked quite extensively about this. As a domestic investor, you have a couple of schemes and special accounts allotted to you by the government especially to enable you to invest abroad. You can use these your advantage. Let's look at these more closely.

Liberalized Remittance Scheme (LRS)

The RBI grants you a foreign currency spending allowance each year under the Liberalized Remittance Scheme. According to this, an Indian can currently invest up to US $2,50,000 abroad in a single financial year (April to March). The remittances can be in any currency equivalent to US $250,000 in a financial year. LRS funds can be used for investing in shares, securities, bonds and mutual funds abroad.

You can also open and maintain foreign currency accounts with banks outside India for any of these transactions. These funds can be used to give gifts or donations abroad but they cannot be used to purchase real estate in a foreign country; nor can you use these funds to invest in things like lottery tickets. Another point to be noted is that you are not allowed to remit money to certain countries like Bhutan, Nepal, Mauritius and Pakistan.[14]

A great way of using your LRS allowance is to invest it in alternative assets that are not available to you in India – foreign art investments, or rare stamps and documents.

Do remember that these permissions are subject to the whims of the RBI. In 2013, the RBI brought the LRS limit down to US $75,000 in an effort to curb the fall of the rupee. However, it increased this again to the current limit of US $2,50,000 after reviewing the current financial scenario.

Resident Foreign Currency (RFC) Account

These accounts are meant for NRIs returning to India who need to bring back foreign currency from their overseas bank accounts. An RFC account is a bank account that can be opened by an NRI who returns to India for permanent settlement after staying abroad for a minimum period of one year.

It can be opened as a savings or term-deposit account, and can be held on singly or jointly in the names of those who are eligible. These accounts are also eligible to hold foreign currency and, following the NRI's return, they can have cash inflow from transactions such as sales proceeds of overseas assets and pension received from abroad.

The biggest benefit of an RFC account is that you can use your RFC funds for remittances or investment abroad. Of course, you can also use these funds for expenses and investments in India but it is more prudent to do that through your regular savings account. The only drawback is that you cannot avail any loans against this account.[16]

Non-resident Ordinary (NRO) Account

NRIs and Persons of Indian Origin (PIOs) can open and maintain different types of accounts without special permission from the RBI.[17] One of these accounts is the NRO account. The NRO account can be opened as a current, savings or fixed deposit account.

You can use this account for transferring money from a rupee account of a foreign bank or from payments received in permitted currency from foreign funds or assets. You can also use this account to receive income from various sources such as dividends, pensions, interest or income from the sale of any financial assets, including immovable property or through legacy or inheritance.

You should also know that the funds in these accounts can be used to pay legitimate dues in India, like rent.

Non-resident External (NRE) Account

These accounts, too, can be opened as savings, current, recurring or fixed deposit accounts. However, they must be opened by the non-resident herself and not through the holder of a power of attorney. Interestingly, the money held in the NRE account can be sent back to the overseas account where it came from.

Apart from these accounts and schemes, you can expose your portfolio to foreign investments by investing in feeder funds. A feeder fund is an investment fund which does its investments through a master fund but does not necessarily invest in exchange traded securities This is a great option because feeder funds invested in India offer exposure to both developed as well as emerging markets like China and those of the Association of South East Asian Nations (ASEAN). As an investor, this is a very promising bargain for you since you can get the best of both worlds. The best way to access these funds is through asset management companies.

Your Money Mantra

When you are investing in local markets, you have a number of options to choose from, but when it comes to exposing your portfolio to a global market your choices will be limited. Now you must combine these methods to work out a strategy that yields the maximum benefit to you.

- Invest in a feeder fund that has investments in both developed and emerging markets. This will balance the risk-returns proportion of your portfolio.
- Utilize your LRS to invest in alternative assets such as rare documents, stamps or an international art piece. This will further diversify your portfolio.

STEP 4

Getting to Know the global markets

NOW THAT YOU HAVE MADE YOUR WAY TO THE GLOBAL MARKETS, you must familiarize yourself with certain concepts.

Let's start by defining what a ***financial centre*** is. A financial centre is essentially the nerve centre of an economy, a global city that is home to a large number of internationally significant banks, businesses and stock exchanges.[17] An international financial centre has at least one major stock market and is generally considered to be an important participant in international financial market trading.

Historically, the cities of London and New York, with their famous financial houses, have vied for the top spot among the world's leading financial centres. But, over the past few decades, these traditional hotspots have been challenged by the rise of new financial powerhouses in different parts of the globe. Asian financial centres have risen significantly in the last few years and are believed to be the focus of new worldwide growth – especially those in Hong Kong, Singapore, Tokyo and Shenzen.

The Global Financial Centres Index (GFCI) ranks the financial centres based on over 26,000 financial-centre assessments from an online questionnaire, together with over 80 indices from organizations like the World Bank, the Organization for Economic Co-operation and Development (OECD) and the Economist Intelligence Unit.[18]

The ranking has been developed based upon five key areas: people, business environment, market access, infrastructure and general competitiveness.

Top 10 financial centres as of March 2015

Rank	Centre	Country
1	New York	United States
2	London	United Kingdom
3	Hong Kong (SAR)	China
4	Singapore	
5	Tokyo	Japan
6	Zurich	Switzerland
7	Seoul	South Korea
8	San Francisco	United States
9	Chicago	United States
10	Boston	United States

As mentioned earlier, one of the critical components that defines a financial centre is the existence of a major stock market. As you know by now, this is where all the financial trading take place.

Here are some of the largest stock exchanges in the world.

New York Stock Exchange (NYSE)

Headquarters: New York City

This is the largest stock exchange in the world both in terms of market capitalization and trade value. The NYSE is the premier listing venue for the world's leading large and medium-sized companies. It offers a broad array of financial products and services: in cash equities, futures, options, exchange-traded products (ETPs), bonds, market data and commercial technology solutions.

NASDAQ OMX

Headquarters: New York City

This is the second-largest stock exchange in the world in terms of market capitalization and trade value. The exchange is owned by the NASDAQ OMX Group which also owns and operates 24 markets, three clearing houses and five central securities depositories supporting equities, options, fixed income, derivatives, commodities, futures and structured products. It is home to approximately 3,400 listed companies.

Tokyo Stock Exchange (Nikkei)

Headquarters: Tokyo

This is the third-largest stock exchange market in the world by the aggregate market capitalization of its listed companies. It has

2,292 companies which are separated into three sections, the First Section for large companies; the Second Section for mid-sized companies; and the Mothers Section for high-growth start-up companies.

London Stock Exchange (LSE)

Headquarters: London

This is the oldest and fourth-largest stock exchange in the world. It is the most international of all the world's stock exchanges, with around 3,000 companies from over 70 countries trading on its markets. The LSE runs several markets for listing, giving the opportunity to different sized companies to list. For the bigger companies, there is the Premium Listed Main Market; for small and medium enterprises the stock exchange operates the Alternative Investment Market; and for international companies that fall outside the European Union (EU) it operates the Depository Receipt Scheme as a way of listing and raising capital.

Shanghai Stock Exchange (SSE)

Headquarters: Shanghai

This is the world's fifth-largest stock market, and one of the two stock exchanges operating independently in the People's Republic of China. The SSE is not entirely open to foreign investors due to the tight capital account controls by Chinese authorities. The securities listed at the SSE include the three main categories of stocks, bonds and funds. Bonds traded on the SSE include treasury bonds, corporate bonds and convertible corporate bonds.

Hong Kong Stock Exchange (HSE)

Headquarters: Hong Kong

The third-largest stock exchange in Asia, HSE is the sixth-largest in the world in terms of market capitalization. With 1,477 listed companies, it operates a securities market and a derivatives market in Hong Kong with clearing houses for each.

How do you invest in global markets?

To expand your portfolio, you can invest in financial securities in any of these markets. These might be stocks, bonds, mutual funds or index products offered through any of these exchanges. Even if you are not specifically interested in buying index products, it is a good idea to have an understanding of what these are.

Why do you need to keep an eye on these foreign stock indices?

Deborah Yang, Managing Director and Head of the MSCI Index, EMEA, says, '*It is critical for investors to keep track of stock index performance as a key indicator of the fundamental health of a country's economy. Keeping track of foreign stock indices provides the investor with a much broader perspective, allowing her to compare the performance of the domestic Indian market with that of the rest of the world*.'

Just like the Sensex and the Nifty in India, international index products comprise the biggest stocks in other countries. Looking at them will give you a good idea of the current position of the world markets.

WHAT THE EXPERTS SAY

Which foreign indices should the Indian investor be regularly aware of and how?

'The best indices to follow should be ones that are truly representative of global equity index – one that accurately reflects the performance of the markets it covers. MSCI is the leading provider of global equity indices and launched the first global equity index family over 40 years ago.

The most often tracked global indices are the MSCI World, representing developed markets, and MSCI Emerging Markets Indices. The combination of these two indices comprises the MSCI All Country World Index (ACWI). These global indices are used by thousands of investment managers to measure the performance of their funds around the world.

The Indian female investor can also track the performance of these indices, as well as MSCI country and industry subcomponents on MSCI's website (www.msci.com) or in the Indian media.'

– **Deborah Yang**
Managing Director and Head of the MSCI Index, EMEA

Understanding the domino effect of global financial events

A short while ago we highlighted the example of Sherie, who lost a major chunk of her investment by investing abroad. Yes, we did advise you to be prudent while planning your portfolio, but even so, there are factors which are out of your control and can affect your investment adversely. In this chapter, we will explore these factors so that you can temper your enthusiasm for investing with a hint of caution.

One of the major factors that can affect your investments is a financial crisis.

Given that the Indian market is separate from foreign financial markets, you are probably wondering how financial crises originating abroad relate to the economy at home or whether they relate to it at all. The reality is that we live in a tiny world where the performance of the developed economies has a direct and domino effect on what happens to emerging markets like India. which impacts your wealth in rupees.

It's true that Sherie could have done better by keeping her money invested in India, but the situation here wasn't smooth either as there was a drop in the markets due to the economic turbulence in the West.

The most obvious examples of global financial crises (GFC) in the last several years are the ones caused by the US housing market and the collapse of Lehman Brothers, followed by the sovereign debt crisis in Europe. The first started out as a domestic problem in America with large financial houses needing to be bailed out. It led to a systemic liquidity crisis which spread like wildfire, affecting almost everyone across the globe. The sovereign debt crisis that followed soon after, in 2010,[19] was caused by massive government debt in certain European countries like Greece and Spain, which put further stress on the global system.

These are both examples of how the financial system in any country, even India in the future, could go awry. So it's a good idea to understand how a crisis can occur, because one of the basic problems it can lead to is a lack of liquidity in the markets.

How did the GFC affect the Indian investor?

The decrease in credit market functioning in America quickly spread beyond its borders because liquidity, or the ability to raise cash, lies at the heart of the efficient functioning of all financial markets. The freezing of liquidity, in turn, froze a number of credit markets everywhere at a time when interest rates all over the world were steadily rising. Frozen financial markets

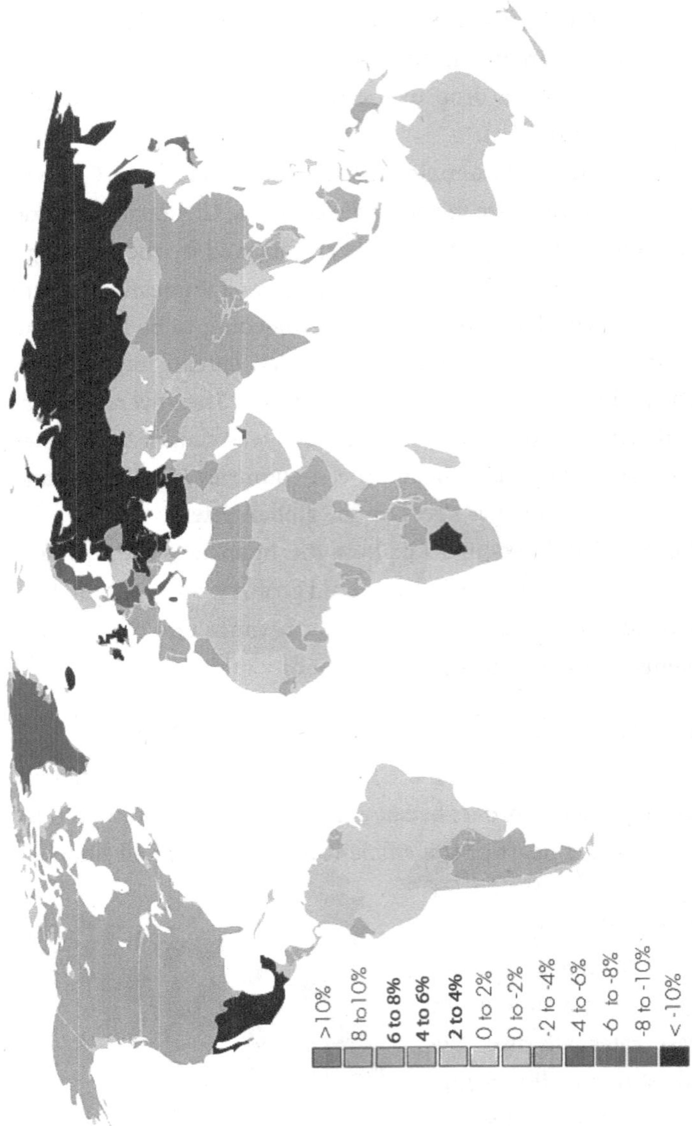

Image showing the real GDP growth rates for 2009 demonstrates the impact of the crisis.

and their subsequent reduction in the rate of lending slowed business investment that subsequently led to a nasty recession all over the globe.

Europe, Asia and emerging markets were all affected and when it came to economic volatility India was no exception. Fear spread through the financial systems across the globe like an epidemic, leading to a sharp decline in asset prices all over the world. In India, the stock market lost at least 50% in 2008 alone. The S&P BSE Sensex went down by more than 10,000 points during that year.[20] It took several years for India to recover – only in 2014 were they able to exceed pre-2008 levels. This span of time was particularly difficult for Indians because investments did not yield suitable returns and high inflation caused a problem in every aspect of life.

Beyond the plummeting stock prices, India experienced other short-term effects of the crisis. Lehman Brothers had outsourced deals to a number of different IT firms, including majors like Tata Consultancy Services (TCS), Satyam Computer Services and Wipro. As a result of the global crisis, the IT sector, too, came under pressure.[21]

It also had an adverse effect on a handful of Indian banks in which the American firm had invested. These local Indian banks had further invested in derivatives, or securities derived from stocks or bonds, and the Indian derivatives market became exposed to the financial shocks abroad.

Public sector banks like Bank of Baroda and ICICI were the worst hit. Luckily, since most local banks did not really have exposure to the troubled assets abroad, the impact on the Indian financial system as a whole was mild.

Nonetheless, investors across the world began to panic.

The finance minister of India at the time, P. Chidambaram, went out of his way to assure people that, unlike in the West, the Indian public sector banks had no exposure to Lehman Brothers. This meant that even though the global credit crunch would impact credit availability in the domestic market, there was no cause for any alarm that Indian banks were vulnerable. SEBI chairman, C.B. Bhave, did the same and the prime minister of India, Dr Manmohan Singh, set up systems to monitor the impact of the global financial crisis on domestic industry.

The good news was that their efforts to allay fear in the Indian investors were not ill-advised and the Indian financial system escaped largely unhurt from the immediate impact of the fall of Lehman as the RBI's historically conservative stance had prevented local banks from taking excessive risk.

The impact of this phenomenon on our economy can be broken down as follows:

- When financial markets are unstable, a sense of fear pervades and, when this happens, investors typically make a flight for gold because it is perceived to be a safe haven for their money. This is exactly what happened in India too. In the aftermath of the financial crisis, increased demand pushed up international gold prices significantly. In India, it was also aided by the weakening of the rupee.
- There was a slowdown in domestic demand and exports. Demand effects were particularly severe in housing, construction, consumer durables and the IT sector.
- The real estate companies funded by Lehman Brothers and its partners were already negatively affected, and the fear that subsequently spread through the financial system made buyers all the more reluctant. So real estate

took a huge hit even though land prices have continued to increase since then.

- There was also a net outflow of foreign capital, a large reduction in foreign reserves and a sharp tightening of domestic liquidity. The outflow of foreign institutional investors (FIIs) from the local equity markets began, as they needed to retrench their assets to cover losses in their home countries. This led to a downward spiral of local stock prices, a depreciation of the rupee and a surge in short-term interest rates. Mutual funds and NBFCs came under pressure due to reduced foreign inflows and subdued capital markets.[22]
- Economic growth decelerated in 2008–09 to 6.7%. This represented a decline of 2.1% from the average growth rate of 8.8% in the previous five years. To counter the negative fallout of the global slowdown on the Indian economy the government responded by rolling out some tax relief measures to boost demand and increased its expenditure on public projects to create employment and public assets.
- Similarly, because the demand for bank credit increased due to dried up foreign sources, the RBI facilitated monetary-easing and liquidity-enhancing measures to help direct funds from the financial system into the productive sectors of the economy.[23]

Economic growth in India did recover after the GFC, but the fact that it was largely fuelled by excess government expenditure has led to higher levels of inflation.

The main outcome of any such crisis is that it leads to a massive liquidity crunch. After the US markets recovered, there was talk of how their government was going to rein in its monetary policy through its 'fed tapering' programme. If that happened, the concern was that it would create problems for India.

Hemindra Hazari, formerly of Nirmal Bang, says, '*Domestic retail investors have been withdrawing their funds from equity mutual funds for some time now, as they have not made much profit in the last five years since the Lehman bust. The fate of the equity markets in India and in other emerging economies which have opened their economies to foreign capital flows is NOT in the hands of domestic investors or fund managers but is determined by foreign flows and by foreign fund managers.*'

'*Foreign capital,*' he emphasises, '*contrary to popular belief or textbook theories, does not flow into efficient market economies but is directed where it seeks profit and exits when it believes profit opportunities are better elsewhere. In the process, however, it creates distortions in the domestic capital markets and economies. Large foreign inflows create stock market booms; stronger domestic currency and high economic growth and large outflows result in bear markets, weaker domestic currency and poor economic growth.*'

Currency Fluctuations

Given such global interconnectedness of economies and the possible impact crises and changes may eventually have an your personal finances, it's important for you to have a basic idea of the various foreign currencies and how the rupee compares to them.

The value of the rupee has fluctuated over the last few years and this can have a positive as well as negative impact on our ability to buy. This becomes especially relevant if you are thinking about investing your LRS allowance in foreign stock markets, where you are exposed to the risk of volatility in currency exchange rates. Say you invest in a dollar fund – if the dollar falls in value vis-à-vis the rupee, then your investment returns will suffer despite the gains your fund may have made in the market. This goes for any foreign currency in which your fund is invested. On the other hand, a fall in the rupee could open up a window of opportunity for Indian investors in things like feeder funds.

The value of the Indian rupee also has an indirect impact on your local stock market investments. When the rupee depreciates, an FII invested in Indian equities will lose money even if the actual price of equities remains unchanged. This is because now, with the same amount of rupees, you get fewer dollars. So even if your rupee investment gains, the equivalent dollar value will not increase unless the returns are more than the fall in rupee against the US dollar, or whatever currency you have converted from. In this scenario, FIIs would be wary of investing in India – nobody wants to invest in a rupee-depreciating environment. But FIIs are huge players in the Indian stock markets and influence them substantially. Hence, their abstinence can arguably subdue stock prices.[24] In the last year or so, FIIs have been pouring money into the system and not surprisingly, equity markets have performed very well in the last year or so.

'*Indian investors investing in Indian assets are not directly exposed to currency fluctuations,*' says Rajeev Malik, senior economist at CLSA. '*I say "directly" as an investor could have an external portfolio. Also, currency changes result in winners and losers – typically, exporters benefit from currency depreciation while companies with import costs suffer. Thus, it is important to keep track of currency changes, especially since greater currency flexibility adopted by emerging markets' central banks, including the RBI, means that it'll be an important parameter which can affect potential returns for investors.*' The massive fall of the Indian rupee against the US dollar in 2014 became an important issue for financial analysts and political leaders alike.

While India is experiencing considerable growth in certain sectors, the story is certainly not as exciting as it was before. You might naturally think that export companies would benefit from a cheaper rupee. In theory yes, but this is largely offset by poor infrastructure, restrictive labour laws and heavy regulation. Our manufacturing sector is stronger than what it was a decade ago, but we still cannot compete with China and other emerging East Asian economies. This means that we rely heavily on imports for materials and equipment that are not available here, and the costs of those imports surge as the rupee falls. All of this impacts our competitiveness, our economy and eventually our financial markets.

So while a weak rupee might be good news for NRI investors who, by sending dollars to India, get more rupees for their dollars, in the overall scheme of things for India and the Indian investor, a weak rupee is not so rosy.

Your Money Mantra

As an investor, be it currency fluctuations or global financial crises, you need to be on the lookout for developments which might affect your investments and then plan ahead.

- Domestic markets in emerging economies like India, which are dependent on foreign cash inflow, are bound to be affected by changes in the global markets.

- The impact might not be felt directly, but its trickle-down effects can be seen in other forms like a high demand for gold, stagnant growth, etc.
- It's important to keep track of currency fluctuations, as they form an important parameter which could affect your potential returns.
- Currency depreciation also results in a regressive financial environment, which further discourages foreign entrants from entering the market. This indirectly affects your portfolio.

Taxes

RELAX, IT'S JUST TAX!

'You must be aware of taxes because they are a major "expense" for all of us. It's wise to understand how these are levied, when we have to pay them and if there are means to reduce our tax expenditure by sensible planning. As a citizen, you should be aware of how the government is using your hard-earned money, which you have contributed in taxes, and hold them accountable, as you hand over almost 30% to 40% of your income in taxes.'

– **Meera Sanyal**
Former CEO and Chairman, Royal Bank of Scotland, India

STEP 1

Tax planning: de-mystifying the process

TAX PLANNING HAS ALWAYS BEEN A MYSTERIOUS DOMAIN. MORE often than not, women rely on their tax planners and chartered accountants to take care of their taxes for them. Not that there is anything wrong with that, but as with other financial decisions you must always be aware of what is happening with your money. In order to familiarize you with the process, we are going to discuss a few basic concepts related to tax planning.

The Fiscal Year

If I ask you about New Year's Day, chances are you'll immediately think about the first day of January or perhaps the day after Diwali. But in the world of taxes, things are a little different. Taxes are calculated according to the 'tax year' which, unlike the calendar year, runs from 1 April to 31 March of the following year. This is also known as a financial year (FY) or a fiscal year.

Regardless of which term you use, they all mean the same thing – the period defined for calculating your taxes, based upon your financial statement for this period. For businesses, it's the period used to calculate the annual performance or close financial statements.

So why is this relevant to you?

Because a number of policies announced by the government affect businesses in a particular FY – usually the one concurrent to the government announcement, or sometimes the next one. And because businesses close their books according to the FY, the income you earn from investing in those businesses – stocks, bonds and so forth – is also accordingly affected during that particular FY.

Categories for assessing a tax payer

According to the Income Tax Act of 1961, there are various categories under which you can be assessed as a payer. Some of them are listed below.

Individual

Under this category, your personal income, which includes various streams of income, such as salary, rental and interest income, etc., is assessed.

HUF

This stands for Hindu Undivided Family, which is essentially an extended family arrangement consisting of multiple generations living under the same roof based on relationships with a common ancestor. The male members are blood relatives and the female members are mothers, wives and unmarried daughters, or widowed relatives. A group of people who are not related in this way cannot file for taxes under this category. Having a property under HUF or filing the returns under HUF doesn't mean that the entire joint family is living together on a particular property.

If you or your family fall under this category, you can include income from property, business, profession and other sources. Income from salary cannot be included in this since it is a personal source of income and does not belong to the group.

We agree that, on the face of it, the idea of the HUF doesn't sound ideal from the perspective of a woman who is aiming to be financially independent. Even then, the HUF can be a good tax-saving tool because it is considered to be a separate legal entity under tax laws. In theory, what this implies is that if your circumstances fulfil the requirements of a HUF you can file two income tax returns, one in your name and one in the name of your HUF. The only hitch is that you will have to maintain these accounts separately.

Other categories

There are other categories, too, such as company, limited liability partnerships (LLPs) and trusts. The first is a corporate category, while LLPs are meant for partnerships between individuals or between corporate entities. Trusts, on the other hand, are non-profit organizations responsible for carrying out charitable activities and their revenue is in the form of donations or contributions for carrying out such activities.

For the purposes of this book, we are concerned only with taxes filed by you as an individual or as part of a HUF.

Types of taxable income

If you are a working woman, your primary source of income might be your salary, but there are other sources that could provide you with some money on a regular basis. All these sources come under scrutiny when you file for your taxes.

Income from salaries

Any income that you receive as salary is taxable although there are various sub-categories of income paid by your employer that are tax-exempt under the rules and limits specified in the Income Tax Act. These sub-categories include leave travel concessions, retirement gratuities, house-rent allowance and reimbursements for official purposes, medical expenses and conveyance allowance.

Your employer deducts a certain amount as TDS (tax deduction at source) from your salary if it exceeds the minimum exemption limit and notifies this in your Form 16, which shows the tax deductions and net salary paid to you. (The Form 16 and other important documents are described and explained later in the chapter.)

Income from property

Any income you earn from leasing land, buildings and furniture is subject to a tax deduction of 10% levied on the gross rent, as long as the tenant is a company or a corporate entity and not an individual. This is applicable if you cross the specified limit prescribed in the latest budget. As a landlord, this income is based on the actual rental value of your property, or the government determined rental value, whichever is greater.

You are also eligible for a standard deduction of 30% to cover repairs and collection charges. Any interest payments relating to loans used for the purchase and construction of the property are also deductible, based on the limits specified in the Income Tax Act. This means that if your rental income is ₹4 lakh you can deduct ₹1.20 lakh from it and then you will have to pay taxes on the remaining ₹2.80 lakh. The corporate entity that has rented the premises from you will deduct tax at source from the rent if it exceeds ₹1.80 lakh a year. This means you will have a tax credit in your tax statement for the year.

As a tenant, you need not deduct tax on rent paid except in very specific cases, like if you are a professional or have your own business and plan to show the rented property as part of your business expenses. In these cases, you will need to deduct tax – but that is only if you are subjected to a tax audit. Tax deduction is the responsibility of the person making the payment as long as the transaction falls under the purview of the Income Tax Act. However, do note that service tax is also applicable on property rentals, subject to the limits defined in the Act. This means that the landlord will probably charge you or your company or business the rental as well as a service tax amount.

Profits and gains of a business or a profession

If you own a business, you are required to pay tax on the income you earn from your business after you have paid your expenses.

This gives you more flexibility from the tax point-of-view, since all business expenses can be claimed and only the net profit will be taxed. In this scenario, you are required to make an income and expenditure or a profit and loss account, giving details of your income and expenses.

Capital gains

Any sale, exchange or transfer of capital assets (such as real estate, shares, bonds, jewellery, paintings or art), which profits you due to an increase in its value from the time you purchased it to the time you transferred or sold it, requires you to pay tax on these profits. This is also referred to as capital gains.

Essentially, there are two types of capital gains:

- ***Short-term***, under which anything held for less than 36 months is subject to a 30% tax (obviously, the effective tax levied will depend on the entire income from all sources and the exemptions available to the individual).
- ***Long-term***, under which anything held for more than 36 months is subject to a 20% tax.

These percentages have been the same for some time now, just like income tax percentages which are standard with changes occurring only in the slabs they apply to.

In addition to this, there are a few assets that are taxed on a long-term basis even if they are held for 12 months or more. These include:

- Company shares
- Government securities
- Listed debentures
- Units of UTI or mutual funds
- Zero-coupon bonds

Income from other sources

Income from certain sources does not come under any of the categories mentioned above but is still taxable.

These include:

- Income from dividends
- Interest from bank FDs and savings accounts
- Income from lottery winnings
- Interest on securities such as debentures, government securities and bonds
- Income from gifts (which falls under the taxable category, as explained below)
- Interest on compensation or enhanced compensation
- Income from renting out assets (for example, cars, jewellery, art)
- Family pension received by family members after the death of the pensioner
- Interest income on things other than securities (for example, interest from loans that you provide others)

Different types of taxes

Given below are the various kinds of taxes levied by the government, which you pay directly.

Income tax

This is the tax you pay the government based on your income in the previous FY. You are charged income tax according to your age and your income. The rule of thumb is that the more you earn, the more tax you pay, and also the older you are, the greater is your chance for tax exemptions. This is because the government recognizes that once you become a senior citizen you are most likely to retire and dip into your savings and investment income in order to maintain your previous lifestyle.

If you are under the age of 60, you have a basic exemption limit of ₹2.50 lakh but anything that you earn over and above this is taxable.

If you are a senior citizen (between the ages of 60 and 80), your annual tax exemption limit is ₹3 lakh, and if you are a super senior citizen above the age of 80 your tax exemption amount goes up to ₹5 lakh. So you pay tax on any amount you earn above these specified amounts.

The exemption limits are subject to surcharges and could change with each year's Union Budget. The amount you pay as income tax depends upon whether that income comes from revenue, like your monthly salary, or from the capital appreciation of your assets. It also depends upon whether you are a resident of India or not.

For the latest income slabs, please see Appendix 4 on p. 302.

Section 56(2)(vii) of the Income Tax Act details particulars related to gifts that are taxable. 'Gifts' here refers to money or property given by one person to another. Gifts given up to a specified limit and from some family members are not subject to tax. However, you need to be aware of the definition of 'relatives' from whom gifts are non-taxable (that is, immediate family only), since gifts from all other people are taxable.

Property tax

As a property owner, the property you own becomes taxable. Property tax rules are subject to a variety of factors, such as the size of the property, the built-up area on the property, and under which category the colony or locality your property is located in falls. (The more upmarket colonies fall in category A, anything below that is in category B, and so on.)

Your Money Mantra

Now that you have a basic understanding of taxation, you can ask pertinent questions to the government about where your money is going and you can also seek measures to save on your taxes.

- Your taxable income will include your income from all resources.
- You can avail tax benefits by applying for tax returns through an individual account as well as a HUF in order to maximize your tax savings.
- There are two types of capital gains, short-term and long-term, and they are subject to different tax percentages.
- The more you earn, the more you have to pay as tax. However, age is also a factor as senior citizens are given a number of tax benefits.
- The rental income that you receive from leasing out your property is liable for taxation though you are eligible to deduct 30% for covering loan payments, repairs and collection charges.

STEP 2

Understanding tax terminology

WHILE OUR EARLIER DISCUSSION SERVES AS A BASIC INTRODUCTION to various aspects of taxation and tax filing, the surefire way to do it right is to sit down with your tax advisor and go over your specific issues in detail. Your tax advisor will be able to tell you how to correctly categorize your income under different headings, the specific exemptions that are more suitable for you, and the best way to file taxes – as an individual, as a married couple or as part of a HUF.

However, you still need to familiarize yourself with the terms used in the tax filing process. Here's a short glossary of the terms used in tax jargon:

TDS

This stands for 'tax deducted at source'. As we've already mentioned, this is a means of collecting tax at the source of income. According to the concept of TDS, the person or institution (such as banks or your employers) charged with such responsibility has to deduct tax at the appropriate rates from payments which are being made to a certain recipient. The deducted sum is then deposited with the relevant authorities. The recipient gets the credit of the amount deducted in her personal assessment on the basis of the certificate issued by the deductor.

PAN Card

This is a permanent account number (PAN), more like a tax identification number to identify and link taxes paid in your name. So if your employers deduct TDS from your salary, they will file a TDS return in your name referencing your PAN number.

Your PAN number shows all the taxes paid by you. At the end of the financial year, all taxes such as TDS and advance tax paid by you will be identified with this number.

26AS Statement

The 26AS statement shows the income earned in the year, which has been taxed and also the tax deducted on this. It is available on the website of the income tax department of the government of India. However, other income like interest from your savings account, where the bank does not cut tax, will not be recorded here. But that does not mean that you should leave it out of your personal income tax return.

TAN (Tax Deduction and Collection Account Number)

This applies more to corporate organizations but certain individuals subject to tax audits also need to apply for a TAN and deduct tax on specified transactions and payments.

Form 16

This is the form issued by an employer to an employee, specifying details like the salary income and its components, the tax deducted by the employer and the tax paid on the earnings from such employment.

Form 16A

This is a non-salary statement of tax deduction and is issued by banks, tenants, etc.

Advance Tax

This is the tax you deposit before the FY ends, in anticipation of the total taxable income for the FY.

Self-assessment Tax

A self-assessment tax is the shortfall that you pay after the year is over and you have computed your total tax liability for the year. So if the total tax paid within the year (up to March) was ₹20,000 but actual amount due (based on your income) turns out to be ₹25,000, you will need to deposit the balance of ₹5,000 as self-assessment tax. The tax which is paid within the year is either TDS or advance tax.

STEP 3

Filing your tax return

LET'S JUST PUT IT OUT THERE – FILING AN INDIVIDUAL RETURN is by no means as scary or complicated as it is made out to be.

For most salaried people, the income streams are quite straightforward. If you have made a large transaction during the year – a property sale or purchase perhaps – it might be a good idea to discuss this with a tax advisor. Otherwise, you can file your tax return online quite easily. The income tax form is quite self-explanatory in terms of what needs to be filed under which head and also comes with detailed guidelines.

The essentials behind filing returns

Here are a few things that you should know about thoroughly before you file your income tax return:

The income that you need to disclose

Be clear on the income you need to disclose. Your salary and house rental allowance (HRA) form the basics, but you will need to mention other components, too (if you have any). These may be rental income, interest income, business income and capital gains.

If you are a salaried employee, you must ask your employer about company policies on reimbursement, as these become part of your total income package. Reimbursements are tax-free and should be given to you as part of your package as long as you submit the required bills for medical expenses, conveyance, uniforms and so on. The tax return form itself is detailed, and will ask all the relevant questions for you to be able to detail these correctly.

The Income Tax Return (ITR) that you have to file

Just as there are various categories for assessing you as a tax payer, there are various types of ITRs that are filed.

ITR-1: The individual income tax return

The ITR-1 Form, also called *SAHAJ* (which means 'elegant' in Hindi), is the income tax return form for salaried individuals who earn their income through a salary or pension, single house property (it excludes cases where loss is brought forward from previous years) and other sources of income, which could include bank interest and fixed deposit interest (excluding other windfall gains like winnings from a lottery or horse races).

This return form cannot be used by a resident who owns any

asset outside India or is a signing authority in any account located outside India.

ITR-2: For individuals/HUFs without income from a business or profession

This ITR applies to individuals and HUFs earning an income through a salary or pension, from property, capital gains, lottery winnings, bets on racehorses and legal forms of gambling.

If the income of your spouse and your dependant needs to be clubbed together, make sure that the source of income is among those stated above. A difference in any category means the assessee will be liable for filing separate returns.

Other forms

There are other forms which are meant for individuals acting as partners or proprietors, for associations of people and for companies and trusts. These forms are regularly changed by the Income Tax department. This could happen every year or once every few years. For example, in the current year, new forms were introduced, due to which the government extended the last date for filing taxes for the current year to 31 August 2015. These new forms include:

ITR 2A, which is meant for individuals and HUFs whose source of income is neither business nor profession and capital gains, and for those who do not hold foreign assets;

ITR 4S (SUGAM), which is meant for individuals or HUFs who have income from presumptive business. 'Presumptive business' means a specific income earned under a special provision of Section 44AE and 44AD of the Act.

The schedule for filing your taxes

Make sure you know in advance the due dates for filing your income tax returns. You should avoid delays as you will be charged interest for both late payment and late filing of the return. If you file a late return, you will not be allowed to revise the return in case you want to do so. However, senior citizens are not required to pay this interest, even if they do not pay advance tax.

The interest charged for late payment of taxes and not filing the return are as below:

- Interest is charged at 1% per month if the tax is not paid according to the defined schedule, based on the computation of amount already paid.
- Interest is charged at 1% if 90% tax is not paid before the end of the FY.

Important dates for filing your return

	Assessee	Date
1.	Any individual/other person (including HUFs, salaried people, business people not covered under audit/tax audit*)	31 July (extended to 31 August for FY 2014–15)
2.	A company	30 September
3.	A person whose accounts are required to be audited	30 September
4.	A working partner of a firm whose accounts are required to be audited	30 September

*A tax audit is required if the income from your business or profession exceeds the specified exemption limit permitted for your category in a year. There are certain corporate assesees whose due date for filing ITR is 30 November.

TDS and Advance Tax: resolve the confusion

As you know by now, TDS is the upfront tax that is deducted on payment if the payment is above the specified limit. TDS makes your tax burden easier to manage since the tax gets paid and recorded in your account through the year so you are not burdened with paying the entire tax amount at the end of the year.

If you are under the age of 60 and have an estimated tax liability of a minimum of ₹10,000, you fall under a category of people who are required to pay advance tax. The advance tax is a certain percentage of your total tax liability for the year and needs to be paid according to defined timelines during the previous year. So you would need to pay a certain percentage as advance tax in 2015 as part of your tax payments for 2016. Everyone who is a tax-payer is required to pay an advance tax.

Due dates of advance tax payment

Assessees other than corporates	Assessees that are companies/ corporates
On or before 15 September – Not less than 30% of advance tax liability.	On or before 15 June – Not less than 15% of advance tax liability.
On or before 15 December – Not less than 60% of advance tax liability, as reduced by the earlier amount paid.	On or before 15 September – Not less than 45% of advance tax liability, as reduced by what is paid earlier.
On or before 15 March – 100% of the advance tax liability, as reduced by what is paid earlier.	On or before 15 December – Not less than 75% of advance tax liability, as reduced by the earlier amount paid.

The documents you need to collect

Collect all necessary documents, such as tax certificates from your banks, employer and other companies well before the due date for filing tax returns so that you have adequate time to prepare them. Generally, your employer is supposed to issue all tax deduction documentation by 31 May after the end of the previous FY on 31 March.

Further, make sure that you match your bank receipts with the information given in the document issued by your employer. It is of paramount importance that there is no disparity between the two.

Similarly, make sure that your 26AS statement matches the documents that your employer issued, namely Form 16 and Form 16A. For reference, you can also download your tax statement from the income tax website by creating an account using your PAN number.

Filing your tax returns online

What is a better way to be financially independent than to file your tax returns on your own?

Now you can fill out your tax returns online, where detailed instructions are given to make the process easier for you. There are, of course, a bunch of websites out there that can help you in filing your returns, but why pay them a fee when it is easy enough to do yourself?

Individuals who earn above a certain amount (see the list of tax brackets below) have to file their taxes.

For individuals – Male/Female (below 60 years), this limit is ₹2.5 lakh

For Senior Citizens (60 to 80 years) – ₹3 lakh
For Very Senior Citizens (above 80 years) – ₹5 lakh

You taxes must be filed by 31 July for the previous year, unless, as we mentioned, you are subject to an audit. Then your cut-off date is 30 September.

Your Money Mantra

Filing taxes is not a complicated process. However, it needs proper management.

- Plan for your taxes with the due dates in mind so that you don't have to pay penalties.
- State all the components of your income clearly and have a ready reference for all exemptions claimed (bills, invoices any other documents).

STEP 4

Your tax-management checklist

✓ State your income clearly

THE AMOUNT OF SALARY YOU HAVE DECLARED SHOULD BE consistent with the amount mentioned in your Form 16 given by the employer and also the 26AS, which is your tax statement. Also, check that the total remuneration mentioned in Form 16 is what you have received in the year. Similarly, all interest income taken from the bank statements or investment statements of an account should match with the 26AS. It is possible that the bank statement has credited more or less than what is there in 26AS – this could be because of different reasons. One, that the savings interest may not be reflected in the 26AS since the bank will deduct TDS from the deposit income. Also, at year-end, the bank might accumulate interest income due till the end of March and while this may not be paid to you within the month of March, it will be recorded in the tax statement as your income.

✓ Maintain records for all the exemptions claimed

Please keep records of all contributions to PPFs, LIC or donations. Since these have to be included in your tax return. If you show business or professional income you will need to maintain an income and expenditure account, and also a profit and loss account. You will need to maintain all invoices and bills for these.

Do note that the Income Tax department has clarified that employers cannot include the tax exemption on donations made to private trusts. It has specified certain trusts (Government trusts, like the Prime Minister's National Relief Fund) that can be accepted by the employer. This, of course, does not mean that you cannot donate to private trusts. Of course you can, but you need to show and account for this in your personal tax returns.

✓ Plan in advance

Always do an estimated income tax computation during the year to ensure that taxes have been paid within the timelines specified in the year, that is, by September, December and March. This will save you from any interest payment that will arise if you default.

✓ Consult a professional

Though we've asked you to file your tax returns on your own it is always better to consult a tax advisor for complicated transactions, like sale of a property, so that the ITR is filed correctly and does not contain any discrepancies. In any case, there is no harm in double-checking.

✓ Make sure there is no disparity between loan payments

If a loan has been taken, always reconcile the loan and interest paid on house property with the statements the bank provides.

Your tax-saving ready reckoner

If you are thinking that in this era of inflation and sky-rocketing prices taxes are going to break your back, then relax – we've got it all covered!

As you know by now, a number of investment schemes and options are tax exempt, though subject to certain limits under Chapter VI(A) of the Income Tax Act. This gives you the opportunity to not only reap high returns on your investments but also save on your taxes. In order to get the most out of this exemption rule, you should plan your investments across asset classes so as to maximize your tax savings. You should also consult with your tax planner or investment advisor in order to know the details of these options and their suitability to your portfolio and utilize the true potential of this scheme. We've listed some of the common and not-so-common forms of tax savings instruments here for your benefit.

Investments that help you save tax

Investment type: *Savings*

National Savings Certificates (NSC)

NSCs are an assured return scheme in which the minimum investment is ₹100 but there is no upper limit as such. A deposit of ₹1.5 lakh in an NSC is eligible for tax rebate. However, this amount is not for individual investment options. Please remember that the interest income earned from this is liable for taxation. All eligible deductions under Section 80 cannot exceed ₹1.5 lakh.

5-Year POTD scheme

POTDs are available for varying time periods but out of those only a 5-year deposit qualifies for tax saving under Section 80C. However, do remember that it is the initial investment that qualifies for the tax rebate. The interest is still taxable.

EPF

Contribution to EPF is eligible for deduction under Section 80C. However, please be aware of the rules of PF for withdrawing the PF amount in less than 5 years and also about the maximum amount that can be withdrawn each year, as these can affect your tax benefits.

PPF/PF

The money put in a PPF or PF is currently eligible for an exemption up to a limit of ₹1.5 lakh (for all investment eligible under Section 80C together). You can claim deductions in respect of PPF contributions made in your own name or for your minor children. This makes it a great savings instrument as well as a great tax saver. However, the total deduction cannot exceed ₹1.5 lakh for you and your family.

Fixed Deposits

Fixed deposits are a safe instrument to invest money in and get returns on interest as high as 9% to 9.25%, depending on the current economic situation and other factors. Bank FDs with a duration of 5 years and tax-saving fixed deposits of scheduled banks with a tenure of 5 years are also entitled for deduction under Section 80C. Before you put your money in these deposits its best to confirm with your bank that the deposits and schemes that they are offering qualify for this deduction as per the conditions specified in Section 80C.

Special Deposits for Senior Citizens

Section 80CCC stipulates that an investment in ***pension funds*** is eligible for deduction. The investment limit for Section 80CCC is clubbed with the limit of Section 80C – this means that the total deduction available for 80CCC and 80C is ₹1.5 lakh. Your investment in pension funds up to a limit of ₹1.5 lakh, can be claimed as a deduction.

Those who have completed 60 years of age can claim deduction under Section 80C for money deposited in an account under the ***Senior Citizen Deposit Scheme***, which has to be maintained for 5 years. But if you withdraw the deposit before 5 years, the amount withdrawn shall become taxable at the time of withdrawal in case deduction has been claimed earlier, though any money received by the nominee or legal heirs on closure of the account before the completion of 5 years due to death of the account holder shall not be taxed.

Investment type: *Hybrid*

Equity Mutual Funds

When it comes to investing your money in tax saving investments, Swati Kulkarni, Executive Vice President and Fund Manager, UTI, tells us that equity mutual funds are a good way to go. '*If the fund is more than 65% into equity-related instruments, then, as per the Indian income tax law, any dividend you get on that is totally tax free. And if you as the investor decide to withdraw your money from the fund after one year, your total capital gains would be tax-exempt too.*' Aside from tax-free funds, UTI offers equity-oriented tax saving funds. '*Up to ₹1 lakh of investment into these funds is tax free,*' says Swati. '*So if your taxable income is X, it always comes down to X– ₹1 lakh if you are invested in a tax saving fund.*' There you go. A simple solution for all your tax problems.

Equity-linked Savings Schemes

An equity-linked savings scheme (ELSS) is a type of mutual fund scheme but it works a little differently from other mutual funds as the money in an ELSS gets locked in for a period of 3 years. Any amount invested in this, up to a limit of ₹1 lakh is tax deductible.

Investment type: *Non-traditional*

Insurance Premium

Any amount that you pay as a life insurance premium for yourself, your spouse or your children can also be included in a

Section 80C deduction. Life insurance premium paid by you for your parents (father, mother or both) is not eligible for deduction under Section 80C. If you are paying premiums for more than one insurance policy then all the premiums can be clubbed together. Payment of premiums for medical insurance also qualifies for tax deductions under Section 80D.

Unit-linked Insurance Plan

Ulips cover is an integrated plan that provides the benefits of life insurance coupled with benefits of equity investments. They are a great option for you, since they not only save tax but also perform well to give you decent returns in the long term.

Expenses that will help you save tax

Education Expenses

Your children's tuition fee is eligible for tax exemption under Section 80C, but under some specific conditions. You can claim the deduction only for two children and that, too, for an educational institution situated in India only. In case you have more than two children, the deduction with respect to other children can be claimed by your spouse, provided your spouse has a taxable income. The deduction is available only for the tuition fee that is to be paid. Any extraneous expenses – donations, for example – cannot be included in this.

EMI Payment

Yes, you read that correctly. This monthly expense can also be accounted for in the tax rebate. The EMI you pay every month for your home loan consists of two components, the principal and the interest. The principal component of the EMI qualifies for deduction under Section 80C. However, there are certain conditions. The deduction can be claimed only if the loan has been taken from certain specified financial institutions or entities like your employer, a public limited company, central government or state government or board, corporation or a university established by law. The claim for deduction can only be made after you have obtained possession of the property, though the repayment might have begun before that. It is also interesting to note that the deduction is available for residential properties only and not for a commercial properties.

Medical Insurance Premium

Payment of your medical insurance premium also qualifies for tax rebate. Currently a deduction of up to ₹25,000 is allowed for yourself (assuming you are the assessee) and your family, as well as for your parent(s). In the case of senior citizens, this limit is ₹30,000.

Other expenses

Section 80DD and Section 80DDB of the Income Tax Act allow you to avail of tax exemptions on expenditure incurred while undergoing medical treatment for yourself or a family member and the care and maintenance of a handicapped dependant.

The Union Budget and you

DECODING THE BUDGET

'In every Union Budget you should analyse how the government is managing its finances, see if it is spending wisely. Figure out how the government's decisions affect you and your family.'

– **Meera Sanyal**
Former CEO and Chairman, Royal Bank of Scotland, India

STEP 1

Understanding the Union Budget

EVERY YEAR, IN FEBRUARY OR MARCH, YOU MUST HAVE FELT THE palpable tension in the air as everyone eagerly awaits the finance minister's latest offering – the Union Budget, or what is referred to in our Constitution as the Annual Financial Statement. The Budget is a powerful tool in the hands of the government as it contains proposals regarding taxes, industrial trade, exchange rate policies and financial sector reforms – all of which can impact the financial markets. It is a detailed document that allocates funds to be spent on various sectors such as defence, education, sports training and special schemes like the Nirbhaya Fund to benefit various sections of our society.

The Budget looks at each sector of the economy and shows you how the government will use its funds to incentivize the development of these sectors through a variety of measures, including tax rebates or manufacturing incentives for specific industries. It also announces policies that affect the development of your portfolio in the financial markets. It's a good idea to thoroughly examine the highlights of the Budget every year to pick and choose the areas that truly affect you. You must know what the government is trying to advocate and what it is trying to dissuade you from, and think about how this fits with your personal goals and objectives.

Until 1992, the Union Budget was a run-the-mill affair, but in the session of 1992–93, finance minister at the time, Manmohan Singh, presented his post-liberalization budget. He opened up the economy by encouraging foreign investments and reducing import duty from over 300% to 50% – a sea change for our country. After this, it was the budget released in July 2014 by Arun Jaitley, the new finance minister of the BJP government, that promised to turn a new leaf for India's growth story. His pro-business budget aimed to catalyse capital markets and create opportunities for the retail investor. This is the perfect time for the modern Indian woman to grow her wealth.

How does it affect you?

Simply speaking, it affects you profoundly because it shows you exactly where you will stand financially over the next 12 months or so.

Let's take the case of the 2015–16 Union Budget.

This was the first complete budget by the current finance minister and it goes without saying that many were disappointed by the lack of big-bang reforms they had been expecting. However, this budget did focus on three key areas – skills and job creation; infrastructure; and rationalization of taxes.

It brought great news for anyone earning income through salary, business or with a plain interest earning assets. This budget was focused on laying out a long-term plan for reform, which is why the current year did not witness any immediate substantial change. Overall, the 2015–16 Union Budget was growth-oriented and it came at a moment when the economy was poised to take off.

Since its independence in 1947, India has had one of the highest running fiscal deficits in the world.

- The government abolished the wealth tax and added a 2% surcharge for the super rich (those with an annual income of over ₹1 crore).
- A sovereign gold bond was announced as an alternative to purchasing metal gold. A new scheme was also initiated for depositors of gold to earn interest and for jewellers to obtain loans on their metal accounts.
- Specifically, it aimed at a GDP of 8–8.5%, an inflation rate of 5%, a realistic fiscal deficit of 3.9% (down from 4.1% in the previous year) and a manageable current account deficit.
- The government allocated ₹70,000 crore ($11 billion USD) and tax-free bonds for rail, road and irrigation projects to boost infrastructure growth. It opened up a wide window of tax-free, fixed investment opportunities, which simply didn't exist before.
- Corporate taxes were slated to be reduced from 30% to 25% over the next four years but service taxes were raised to 14% (awaiting final date of implementation).

- The much awaited Goods and Services Tax integrating the various indirect taxes was slotted for implementation in April 2016.
- Around 2004, only 9,71,182 all-women SHGs had been credit-linked to banks. At the end of December 2013, 41,16,000 women SHGs had been provided credit and the outstanding amount of credit was ₹36,893 crore.
- Another important aspect of this budget was the allotment of ₹1,000 crore to the Nirbhaya fund set up by the UPA government and NGOs to protect women following the infamous gang rape in Delhi in December 2012.
- Other government objectives in this Budget aimed to strengthen the Indian financial markets included the merging of commodities regulators with SEBI and clarity on REIT rules.

How does it affect the markets?

The Budget, while signalling the changes in the economic policy of the country, also has a way of affecting financial markets.

Different analysts have different views on this. Some say that, as far as returns go, budgets have maximum impact in the short-term immediate post-Budget period. Moreover, volatility doesn't really increase in a long-term post-Budget situation.[1] However, some others disagree and argue that it's all about volatility. One study shows, for example, that in the years from 1990 to 2000, April was always the most volatile month for the stock markets, followed by February and March. The author ascribes this volatility to the announcement of the Union Budget in February.[2] Another study shows that stock prices always react fairly quickly to Budget news but, oftentimes, the first correction is not necessarily accurate.[3]

In 2015, the Modi government's first full-year budget turned out to be a volatile affair for stocks. The Sensex swung 700 points initially as investors were disappointed due to lack of big-bang reforms, but then the promise of lower corporate taxes and deferral of the General Anti-Avoidance Rule (GAAR) had a huge impact on the market, bringing it up by 141 points to end at 29,361 by the end of the trading day. The Nifty rose 57 points to finish above the 8,900 level. This was the first time in four years that the Sensex saw an upsurge on a budget day.

Your Money Mantra

The trickle-down effect from the Union Budget can impact you in a number of ways, influencing your capacity as a consumer, as an investor and, most importantly, as a tax payer.

- Be updated and aware of all Union Budget components so that you can evaluate your own budget and plan your finances accordingly.
- Remember that the Union Budget is not only responsible for allocating funds to various sectors but also for propelling the markets to be volatile, both of which will affect your investment decisions for the year ahead.

Demystifying the Union Budget 2015–16

To understand how certain key changes in the Union Budget affect you, follow the signs!

 This will increase your household budget.

 This will decrease your household budget.

Monetizing Gold

The new budget put a great deal of emphasis on monetizing gold, which means that you will have more to spend as well as save for your household.

What this means for you

Think about it. Cash begins to multiply the moment it is converted to a bank deposit. Gold, however, does not pay interest or dividends. Therefore, by earning interest on gold bonds or deposit schemes, your household budget will definitely go up.

Service Tax Hike

The service tax was increased from 12.36% to 14%.

What this means for you

This will impact your daily life as everything from eating out to cosmetics, movie tickets, phone bills, even grocery shopping will become more expensive. All this will mean that your household budget might feel the squeeze.

Mobile Handsets to Become Expensive

The excise duty on imported mobile handsets used to be 1% when the vendor did not claim a central value added tax (CENVAT) and 6% if he did. The latter has now been increased to 12.5% , while the former remains the same.

What this means for you

Handset makers will increase prices by up to 5% after the budget raises excise duty. This will make buying the latest mobile phone an expensive proposition.

Savings

The new budget proposed to revitalize small savings schemes which will help in providing for the education and marriage of a girl child. A National Savings Certificate with an insurance cover was also slated to be launched to provide additional benefits for the small saver.

What this means for you

The more you save, the more you will earn.

Cost of Aerated Drinks

The new budget increased the excise duty on aerated drinks from 17.5% to 18%.

What this means for you

Now cooling off is going to burn your pocket a little more. Prices of cola and packaged water will be raised by ₹1.

Taxes

Small- and mid-income earners will benefit from an additional income tax deduction introduced under Section 80CCD. However, as mentioned earlier, anyone reporting an income of more than ₹1 crore per year will be required to pay a surcharge of 2%.

What this means for you

If you belong to the high income group, a bigger portion of your income will now go into paying your taxes.

Others, though, will be paying less tax which will consequently enhance your household budget.

Benefits

Salaried employees are given a choice in determining how their salaries should be paid out in terms of benefits. They can opt for an Employee Provident Fund (which is optional for employees under a certain income threshold) or a National Pension Scheme and either an employee's state insurance or a health insurance product that is recognized by the Insurance Regulatory Development Authority.

What this means for you

Even though you can choose how you want your benefits allocated, it doesn't increase or decrease your personal budget.

Wealth Tax

The new budget proposes to abolish wealth tax from the FY 2015–16.

What this means for you

You will no longer have to value your taxable assets and file a separate wealth tax return. However, the assets will now have to be disclosed in your income tax return. This means you'll have to value all your jewellery each year and declare it on income tax return form rather than on a separate wealth tax return form. Chances are that the ITR format will be revised to accommodate this change or annexures will be added to go along with it.

Transport Allowance

The exemption limit for transport allowance has been increased to ₹1,600 per month from ₹800 per month.

What this means for you

For a mid-income earner, this will enable tax savings of up to ₹3,322.

Check Your Financial IQ

Take a deep breath and get set to test your newly acquired financial gyaan!

1: What is net profit?

1. All the money you make in addition to your expenses.
2. Gross income, excluding your expenses.
3. Only the money that you earn on an annual basis.

2: What is a share or stock?

1. A large piece of pie.
2. A piece of all the companies of a certain type.
3. Essentially, a portion of ownership of a company or other legal entities.

3: A dividend is ____

1. The money that a bank loans to a company.
2. The money that a company invests in the stock market.
3. A shareholder's portion of the company's profits.

4: What is the definition of market capitalization?

1. The process in which a state controlled economy changes to a capital economy.
2. The product of the number of outstanding shares multiplied by the share price.
3. The time it takes for a company to become a part of the capital economy.

5: What is a stock market?

1. A place where people decide to share the profit they earn from a company.
2. The place where companies meet to discuss how they believe their stocks are doing.
3. A place where company stocks are publicly bought and sold.

6: What does a stock broker do?

1. A stock broker is someone who sells stocks in their own company.
2. A stock broker is any person who likes to buy and sell stocks.
3. A stock broker is someone who buys and sells stocks on your behalf.

7: What are capital gains?

1. The capital city of a country that gains recognition in the financial works.
2. Money that you put in a company.
3. Profit you make from selling assets like stocks and bonds.

8: What is TDS?

1. Total deductible salary.
2. Taxes for daily salary.
3. Tax deducted at source.

9: Which governing body regulates the securities market?

1. RBI
2. NSE
3. SEBI

10: What is an 'investment'?

1. A special kind of secret money.
2. Profits made by a company which are re-invested.
3. Money that you put into companies, hard assets or the financial markets.

11: What is an IPO?

1. An investment public option – when the public is informed who has invested in a company.
2. An initial public opening – when a company first allows the public to buy products.

3. An initial public offering – when a corporation first sells stocks to the public.

12: What is a portfolio?

1. A collection of art and photography.
2. Something you present to a wealth manager in order to hire his services.
3. A collection of investments owned by an investor.

13: What is a bull market?

1. A market when the economy is doing well and the prices of stock tend to rise.
2. A market that is decreasing rapidly.
3. A market that has a bull inside of it.

14: What is a bear market?

1. When the economy is doing poorly and the prices of stocks tend to fall.
2. When the economy is not doing overly well or poorly, i.e. prices of stocks tend to be stagnant.
3. When the economy is strong and prices are growing.

15: What is the Sensex?

1. A stock market index of all the industrial companies in the Indian stock market at the time.
2. A stock market index of 30 well-established and financially sound companies listed on the Bombay Stock Exchange (BSE).
3. A stock market index of the top 5 industrial companies listed on the BSE.

16: Which one of these is main stock market in the US?

1. NYSE
2. NASDIQ
3. DCSE

17: What is an 'emerging market'?

1. A country whose company stocks are listed on a global stock exchange.
2. A country that has some characteristics of a developed market but is not yet a developed market.
3. A market that is not over-developed.

18: What is risk?

1. A measure of chance in any type of financial investment.
2. Something you must do to save your life.
3. A measure to be avoided in any type of financial investment.

19: What do ETFs have in common with mutual funds?

1. One investment purchases a group of assets.
2. They are both low risk investments.
3. They are both tied to an index.

20: What can be learned from Warren Buffet's approach to investing?

1. Pay attention to rumors and pure market price indicators.
2. Sell when the going is good.
3. Use a 'buy and hold' strategy.

ANSWER KEY

1 – 2, **2** – 3, **3** – 3, **4** – 2, **5** – 3, **6** – 3, **7** – 3, **8** – 3, **9** – 3, **10** –3, **11** – 3, **12** – 3, **13** – 1, **14** – 1, **15** – 2, **16** – 1, **17** – 2, **18** – 1, **19** – 1, **20** – 3.

If you got

- 15–20 answers right – Congratulations! You have certainly imbibed your money mantras well. You are on your way to becoming a smart investor by implementing this freshly acquired knowledge.
- 10–15 answers right – Not a bad effort. You have certainly managed to grasp the basics of financial management. Now you just need to put in a little bit of time and effort to brush up your knowledge.
- Less than 10 answers right – Chances are you regard 'finance' as the 'f-word' and avoid it at all costs. But, relax, just give this book another read. The next time around, you'll have it down pat.

The good news is that whatever your level of financial literacy might be, you will get there with time and practise. With this book, you have taken the first steps in that direction; now you just need to follow through.

List of Resources

Here is a list of resources that you might find useful in expanding your financial literacy.

Aside from the government websites listed here, please note that we are not specifically recommending any of the resources. They are merely listed as references.

Please also note that this is not an exhaustive list by any means. It is always good to expand your lists by doing your own research.

Financial Regulatory Websites

Association of Mutual Funds in India (AMFI)
http://www.amfiindia.com

Government of India – Union Budget
http://www.indiabudget.nic.in

National Institute of Securities Markets
http://www.nism.ac.in.

Reserve Bank of India (RBI)
http://www.rbi.org.in/home.aspx

SEBI Investor Awareness website
http://www.investor.sebi.gov.in

Securities and Exchange Board of India (SEBI)
http://www.sebi.com

PrintWorld Directory
http://www.printworlddirectory.com

Commodities Exchanges

Indian Commodity Exchange Limited (ICEX)
http://www.icexindia.com

Multi Commodity Exchange (MCX)
http://www.mcxindia.com

National Commodity and Derivative Exchange of India (NCDEX)
http://www.ncdex.com

National Multi Commodity Exchange of India Limited (NMCE)
http://www.nmce.com

Stock Exchanges

Bombay Stock Exchange of India Ltd. (BSE)
http://www.bseindia.com

National Stock Exchange of India Ltd. (NSE)
http://www.nseindia.com

Stock Brokers

ICICI Direct
http://www.ICICIDirect.com

HDFC Bank
http://www.hdfcsec.com

Karvy
http://www.karvyonline.com

Kotak Securities
http://www.kotaksecurities.com

Motilal Oswal
http://www.motilaloswal.com

Reliance Securities
http://www.rsec.co.in

SBI Cap Securities
http://www.sbicapsec.com

Share Khan/India Bulls
http://www.sharekhan.com

Sharemaster India
http://www.sharemasterindia.com

Zerodha
http://www.zerodha.com

Financial Advisers/Wealth Managers

B.T.S. Asset Management
http://www.btsmanagement.com

Bajaj Capital
http://www.bajajcapital.com

Client Associates
http://www.clientassociates.com

D.S.P. Merrill Lynch
http://www.dspml.com

Go 4 Advisory Services
http://www.go4advisory.com

P. N. Vijay Financial Services Private Limited
http://www.askpnvijay.com

Paar Tax and Investments Consultants (PTIC)
http://www.pticindia.com

River Bridge Investment Advisors
http://www.riverbridge.in

Unit Trust of India Investment Advisory Services
http://www.utiias.com

Ways2Capital
http://www.ways2capital.com

Wealth Wires Financial Services
http://www.wealthwires.com

Asset Management Companies (Mutual Funds)

Birla Sun Life Mutual Fund
http://www.mutualfund.birlasunlife.com

Franklin Templeton Investments
http://www.franklintempletonindia.com

HDFC Mutual Fund
http://www.hdfcfund.com

ICICI Prudential Asset Management
http://www.icicipruamc.com

Kotak Asset Management
http://www.assetmanagement.kotak.com

Reliance Capital Asset Management
http://www.reliancecapital.co.in

SBI Funds Management Pvt. Ltd.
http://www.sbifunds.com

Tata Mutual Fund
http://www.tatamutualfund.com

UTI Mutual Fund India
http://www.utimf.com

Tax Websites

Clear Tax
http://www.cleartax.in

Delhi Government Property Tax
http://www.delhi.gov.in/wps/wcm/connect/DoIT/delhi+govt/taxes/property+tax

Income Tax Department of India
http://www.incometaxindia.gov.in

Tax Guru
http://www.taxguru.in/income-tax/beginers-guide-income-tax-faq.html

Tax India Online
http://www.taxindiaonline.com/RC2/index.php3

Tax Spanner
http://www.taxspanner.com/

Art Websites

Artshare
http://www.artshree.com

Asian Art Dealers
http://www.asianart.com

Christies (Auction house)
http://www.christies.com

Collins & Kent International
http://www.collinskent.com.au

Saffronart (Auction house)
http://www.saffronart.com

Housing and Real Estate

99 Acres
http://www.99acres.com

Brick Eagle Portal for Affordable Housing
http://www.brickeagle.com

Magic Bricks
http://www.magicbricks.com

National Housing Bank
http://www.nhb.org.in

NHB housing India Info
http://www.housingindia.info

Real Estate India
http://www.realestateindia.com

Gold and Precious Metals

Bullion India
http://www.bullionindia.in

Indian Bullion Market Association
http://www.ibma.co.in

Pushpak Bullions Pvt. Ltd.
http://www.pushpakbullions.com

Financial Portals/Research

Epic Research
http://www.epicresearch.co

India Info Online
http://www.indiainfoline.com

India Notes
http://www.indianotes.com

Insurance Mall
http://www.insurancemall.in

Apna Paisa
http://www.ApnaPaisa.com

Money Control
http://www.MoneyControl.com

My Iris
http://www.myiris.com

NDTV Profit
http://www.NDTVProfit.com

Rupee Times
http://www.RupeeTimes.com

Rediff.com
http://www.rediff.com

Value Research Online
http://www.ValueResearchOnline.com

Appendices

Appendix 1a

TOP LIFE INSURANCE POLICIES IN INDIA

Insurer	Name of policy
Bajaj Allianz	iGain III Insurance Plan i-Secure Insurance Plan CashRich Insurance Plan
Birla Sun Life Insurance	BSLI Wealth Plan BSLI Guaranteed Wealth
HDFC Standard Life Plan	Click2Protect Online Protection Plan HDFC Life Smart Woman Plan
ICICI Prudential Life Insurance	ICICI Pru iCare
ING Life Insurance	ING Market Shield ING Star Life
Life Insurance Corporation of India	Jeevan Ankur Jeevan Akshay VI
MetLife India	Met Monthly Income Plan

Kotak Life Insurance	Kotak Ace Investment Plan Kotak Assured Income Plan
Tata AIA Life Insurance	Tata AIA Life Insurance Suraksha Kosh Tata AIA Life Insurance Maha Raksha Supreme
Aviva Life Insurance	Aviva iLife
Sahara Life Insurance	Sahara Vatsalya Jeevan Bima
Shriram Life Insurance	ShriLife Wealth Plus Money Back Shriram Ujjwal Life SP
Bharti AXA Life Insurance	Bharti AXA Life eProtect
Future Generali	Future Generali Smart Life
IDBI Federal Life Insurance	IDBI Federal Termsurance Seniors Insurance Plan IDBI Federal Wealthsurance Milestone Plan IDBI Federal Childsurance Dreambuilder Insurance Plan IDBI Federal Lifesurance Suvidha Savings Insurance Plan IDBI Federal Hospitalization and Surgical Plan IDBI Federal Incomesurance Endowment & Money Back Plan IDBI Federal Loansurance Group Life Plan IDBI Federal Homesurance Protection Plan

	IDBI Federal Bondsurance Advantage Insurance Plan IDBI Federal Group Microsurance Plan
Canara HSBC OBC Life Insurance	Dream Smart Plan Secure Smart Plan Grow Smart Plan Smart Sanchay Plan Future Smart Plan
AEGON Religare Life Insurance	iTerm
DLF Pramerica Life Insurance	Wealthassure

Appendix 1b

TOP GENERAL INSURANCE POLICIES

Insurer	Insurance product
Bajaj Allianz General Insurance	Car Insurance Policy CashRich Retirement Plan
ICICI Lombard General Insurance	The Travel Insurance
New India Assurance	The Standard Fire and Special Perils Policy The Householder's Policy The Motor Policy
Oriental Insurance	The Motor Insurance Policy
Reliance General Insurance	The Motor Insurance Policy
Tata AIG General Insurance	Tata AIG Motor Insurance Tata AIG Travel Insurance Tata AIG Wellsurance Family

Shriram General Insurance	Fire Insurance Motor Insurance Engineering Insurance Liability Insurance
Bharti AXA General Insurance	Bharti AXA Car Insurance

Appendix 2a

MUTUAL FUND FACT SHEET

Report as of 3 Jun 2015

ABCD Balanced Fund Growth

Morningstar® Category Index	Fund Benchmark	Morningstar Rating™	Morningstar® Category
-	CRISIL Balanced Fund	QQQQQ	India OE Balanced - Moderate Allocation

Investment Objective

The primary objective of the Scheme is to generate capital appreciation along with current income form combined portfolio of equity & equity related and de & money market instruments.

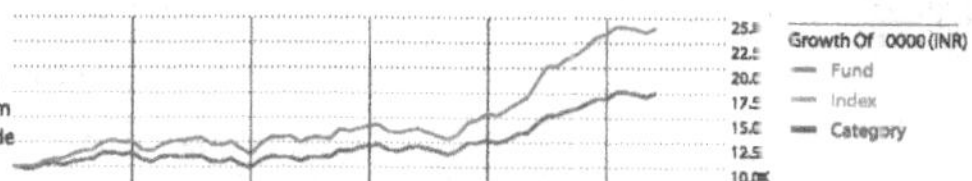

2010	2011	2012	2013	2014	05/15	Performance
25.49	-10.57	26.56	8.78	51.47	2.53	Fund
-	-	-	-	-	-	+/- Index
11.41	2.83	3.23	4.00	16.88	-1.19	+/- Category
5	36	31	13	9	78	Percentile Rank

Risk Measures			
3-Yr Alpha	-	3-Yr Sharpe Ratio	1.35
3-Yr Beta	-	3-Yr Std Dev	11.47
R-Squared	-	3-Yr Risk	abv avg
Information Ratio	-	5-Yr Risk	abv avg
Tracking Error	-	10-Yr Risk	Avg

Trailing Returns (2 Jun 2015)	Return %	+/-Idx	+/-Cat
3 Months	-3.47	-	-0.01
6 Months	1.74	-	-0.12
1 Year	24.21	-	5.57
3 Years Annualised	24.14	-	5.41
5 Years Annualised	16.95	-	5.42

Quarterly Returns	1st qtr	2nd qtr	3rd qtr	4th qtr
2015	2.04	-	-	-
2014	6.59	22.49	5.99	9.46
2013	-5.12	0.06	-1.43	16.24
2012	15.74	-0.40	6.66	2.94
2011	-2.90	5.00	-5.08	-7.60

Portfolio 30 Apr 2015

Asset Allocation	% Long	% Short	% Net
Stocks	68.82	0.00	68.82
Bonds	27.07	0.00	27.07
Cash	4.11	0.00	4.11
Other	0.00	0.00	0.00

Morningstar Style Box™

Equity Style

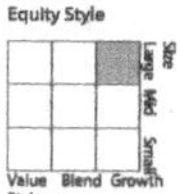

Fixed Income Style

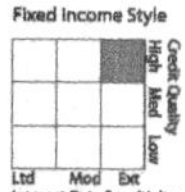

Appendix 2b

THE GOLD EXCHANGE TRADING FUNDS LISTED ON THE NSE

Scheme Name	Symbol	Objectives	Managed By
Axis Gold ETF	AXISGOLD	To generate returns that are in line with the performance of gold.	Axis Mutual Fund
Goldman Sachs Gold Exchange Traded Scheme	GOLDBEES	To provide returns that, before expenses, closely correspond to the returns provided by domestic price of gold through physical gold.	Goldman Sachs Mutual Fund
UTI GOLD Exchange Traded Fund	GOLDSHARE	To endeavour to provide returns that, before expenses, closely track the performance and yield of gold. However, the performance of the scheme may differ from that of the underlying asset due to racking error. There can be no assurance or guarantee that the investment objective of UTI-Gold ETF will be achieved.	UTI Mutual Fund
HDFC Gold Exchange Traded Fund	HDFCMFGETF	To generate returns that are in line with the performance of gold, subject to tracking errors.	HDFC Mutual Fund
ICICI Prudential Gold Exchange Traded Fund	IPGETF	ICICI Prudential Gold Exchange Traded Fund seeks to provide investment returns that, before expenses, closely track the performance of domestic prices of gold derived from the LBMA AM fixing prices.	ICICI Prudential Mutual Fund

Kotak Gold Exchange Traded Fund	KOTAKGOLD	To generate returns that are in line with the returns on investment in physical gold, subject to tracking errors.	Kotak Mutal Fund
Quantum Gold Fund (an ETF)	QGOLDHALF	To provide returns that, before expenses, closely correspond to the returns provided by the domestic price of gold.	Quantum Mutual Fund
Reliance Gold Exchange Traded Fund	RELGOLD	To provide returns that closely correspond to returns provided by the price of gold through investment in physical gold (and gold-related securities as permitted by regulators from time to time). However, the performance of the scheme may differ from that of the domestic prices of gold due to expenses and or other related factors.	Reliance Mutual Fund
Religare Gold Exchange Traded Fund	RELIGAREGO	To generate returns that closely correspond to the returns provided by investment in physical gold in the domestic market, subject to tracking errors.	Religare Mutual Fund
SBI Gold Exchange Traded Scheme	SBIGETS	To seek to provide returns that closely correspond to returns provided by the price of gold through investment in physical gold. However, the performance of the scheme may differ from that of	SBI Mutual Fund

		the underlying asset due to tracking errors.	
Birla Sun Life Gold ETF	BSLGOLDETF	The investment objective of the scheme is to generate returns that are in line with the performance of gold, subject to tracking errors.	Birla Sun Life Mutual Fund
IDBI Gold Exchange Traded Fund	IDBIGOLD	To invest in physical gold with the objective of replicating the performance of gold in domestic prices. The ETF will adopt a passive investment strategy and will seek to achieve the investment objective by minimizing the tracking errors between the fund and the underlying asset.	IDBI Mutual Fund
Motilal Oswal Most Shares Gold ETF	MGOLD	The investment objective is to provide return by investing in gold bullion.	Motilal Oswal Mutual Fund
Canara Robeco Gold Exchange Traded Fund	CRMFGETF	The investment objective is to generate returns that are in line with the performance of gold, subject to tracking errors.	Canara Robeco Mutual Fund

Appendix 3

MSCI LIST OF FRONTIER MARKETS

Here's a current list of countries that MSCI defines as 'frontier markets'. Only 26 of them are a part of the MSCI Frontier Index. The ones marked with an asterisk (*) are not.

ARGENTINA
BAHRAIN
BANGLADESH
BOSNIA-HERZEGOVINA*
BOTSWANA*
BULGARIA
CROATIA
ESTONIA
GHANA*
JAMAICA*
JORDAN
KAZAKHSTAN
KENYA
KUWAIT
LEBANON
LITHUANIA
MAURITIUS
MOROCCO
NIGERIA
OMAN
PAKISTAN
PALESTINE*
ROMANIA
SAUDI ARABIA*
SERBIA
SLOVENIA
SRI LANKA
TRINIDAD & TOBAGO*
TUNISIA
UKRAINE

UNITED ARAB EMIRATES
VIETNAM
ZIMBABWE*

Appendix 4

INCOME TAX

Net income range (individual resident below 60/or any NRI/ HUF)	Net income range (for resident Senior Citizen)	Net income range (for Super Senior Citizen)	Net income range for any other person (excludes companies and co-operative societies)	Income Tax rates
Up to ₹250,000	Up to ₹300,000	Up to ₹500,000	Up to ₹250,000	NIL
₹250,001-5,00,000	₹3,00,001-5,00,000	–	₹2,50,001-5,00,000	10%
₹5,00,001-1,000,000	₹5,00,001-1,000,000	₹5,00,001-1,000,000	5,00,000-₹1,000,000	20%
Above ₹1,000,000	Above ₹1,000,000	Above ₹1,000,000	Above ₹1,000,000	30%

*** *These slabs are subject to surcharges as defined and also expected to change with each year's budget.

References and Endnotes

Growing Your Money

1. http://finance.fortune.cnn.com/2012/02/09/warren-buffett berkshire-shareholder-letter
2. http://daslee.me/warren-buffetts-definition-of-investing
3. http://www.harmonyindia.org/hportal/VirtualPageView.jsp?page_id=67
4. http://health.india.com/diseases-conditions/world-heartday-2013-heart-disease-kills-one-in-three-women
5. Accessed from http://www.harmonyindia.org/hportal/VirtualPageView.jsp?page_id=
6. http://business.rediff.com/report/2009/may/15/perfintypes-of-life-insurance.html

Planning Your Portfolio

1. http://www.slideshare.net/subhankar2105/nse-nifty-calculations
2. http://www.crisil.com/ratings/faqs.html
3. http://crisil.com/ratings/faqs.html#1
4. http://businesstoday.intoday.in/story/iinvest-in-tax-free-bonds-to-get-higherpost-tax-returns/1/190110.html
5. http://law.incometaxindia.gov.in/dittaxmann/incometaxacts/2008itact/sec_010(23d).htm)

Illiquid Investments

1. http://www.gotgoldreport.com/2011/08/grubb-indian-women-holdmore-gold-than-the-us-government.html#sthash.loJaZiGM.dpuf
2. http://www.bullionindia.in/welcome-to-bullion-india
3. http://www.livemint.com/Money/p7QyTErJ0uxzW1DQcSiATN/Reits-Asolution-to-many-problems-in-Indian-real-estate.html
4. http://www.telegraph.co.uk/property/propertypicturegalleries/8892109/In-pictures-The-worlds-20-most-expensive-cities-to-buy-property.html?image=19
5. edition.cnn.com/2014/01/05/.../rocketing-property-prices-in-india/
6. http://www.joneslanglasalle.co.in/ResearchLevel1/APPD_3Q_2013.pdf
7. http://timesofindia.indiatimes.com/business/india-business/Indian-rentalreturns-among-lowest-globally/articleshow/ 25779851.cms
8. *An Art Investment Guide* by Collins & Kent International.

Globalizing Your Portfolio

1. http://www.investopedia.com/terms/e/emergingmarketeconomy.asp

2. http://www.kpmgfamilybusiness.com/business-emerging markets- south-america-china
3. http://www.goldmansachs.com/korea/ideas/brics/buildingbetter-pdf.pdf
4. http://www.content.gs.com/japan/ideas/brics/buildingbetterpdf.pdf
5. http://www.usindiafriendship.net/viewpoints1/Indias_Rising_Growth_Potential.pdf
6. http://timesofindia.indiatimes.com/india/BRIC-nationsfacing-inadequate-supply-of-affordable-housing/articleshow/33086476.cms
7. http://www.livemint.com/Specials/pZRVIsRmoxiNgXhbS65xzJ/The-global-financial-crisis-four-myths-and-a-question.html
8. http://www.goldmansachs.com/korea/ideas/brics/buildingbetter-pdf.pdf
9. http://www.personalfn.com/tools-and-resources/mutualfunds
10. http://www.personalfn.com/tools-and-resources/mutualfunds/#SchemeFinder/SchemeDetailsPage.aspx?SchemeID=6b192d53-2277-4ded-9839-b46fe15f395e%7CKotak%20Global%20Emerging%20Market%20Fund#.U2C0IRZWJSo
11. http://www.bloomberg.com/video/78312296-investing-incambodia-haiti-bangladesh-laos.html
12. https://www.franklintempleton.com/forms-literature/download/096-FF
13. http://www.sanlam.co.za/wps/wcm/connect/5e977c0044a80fb3b612fe45efac8a19/Sanlam+Africa+Frontier+Markets+Feb+2014+FS.pdf?MOD=AJPERES&CACHEID=5e977c0044a80fb3b612fe45efac8a19
14. http://articles.economictimes.indiatimes.com/2012-08-20/news/33287959_1_remittances-lrs-foreign-currency-accounts
15. http://articles.economictimes.indiatimes.com/2013-01-17/news/36394155_1_term-deposit-fcnr-nre

16. https://www.investmentyogi.com/transfer-from-nroaccounts-to-nre-accounts
17. http://www.iongfinance.net/images/GFCI15_15March2014.Pdf
18. http://www.zyen.com/research/gfci.html
19. http://www.bankrate.com/finance/economics/european sovereigndebt-crisis-causes.aspx
20. http://www.livemint.com/Money/3egfzj7LmEOoflsB4RVJ1N/Indian-householdslife-after-Lehman.html
21. http://www.rediff.com/money/2008/sep/16slde14.html
22. http://www.livemint.com/Specials/Jz0STkDuhEehFlOb6kVfoM/How-Indias-banking-sector-weathered-the-global-storm.html
23. http://globalcenters.columbia.edu/content/global-fi nancialcrisis-its-impact-india-and-policy-response
24. www.livemint.com/Money/bUSLL8QApuqXrh5wDY0q5J/How-a-falling-rupee-affects-your-wallet.html

The Union Budget and You

1. Gupta, Arindam and Kundu, Debashish, 2006, 'A study of the impact of Union budgets on stockprices in India'", *The ICFAI Journal of Applied Finance*, Vol. 12, No. 10, pp. 65–76
2. Kaur, Harvinder, 2004, 'Stock Market Volatility in India', *The Indian Journal of Commerce*, Vol. 57, No. 4, pp. 55–70
3. Mohanty, Munmun, 2004, 'Stock Market Reaction to Announcement of Policy Changes', *The ICFAI Journal of Applied Finance*, December 2004.

Appendix

1. http://business.mapsofindia.com/insurance/life-insurance.html
2. http://www.msci.com/products/indexes/country_and_regional/fm/
3. http://www.valueresearchonline.com/funds/repcard.asp

Acknowledgements

TO SAY THAT THIS BOOK HAS BEEN A LONG AND ARDUOUS JOURNEY would be a complete understatement. But all journeys begin with a single step and become a treasure trove of wonderful experiences thanks to all you encounter along the way.

This particular journey would not have been possible without the support of our family, our colleagues and friends.

To our parents, Anita and Vinod Vij, Veena and R.K. Malhotra, thank you for encouraging us in all of our pursuits and inspiring us to follow our dreams.

To our life partners, Sumchit Anand and Neeraj Hora, thank you for dealing with our bouts of crabbiness throughout this writing journey.

To all of the contributors, thanks for your time, energy and expertise: Kalpana Morparia; Usha Ananthasubramanian, CMD, Bharatiya Mahila Bank; Naina Lal Kidwai, Group General Manager and Country Head, HSBC India; Suresh Soni, CEO, Deutsche Asset Management India Pvt. Ltd; Kapil Mehta, Managing Director, Secure Now Insurance Broker Pvt. Ltd.; Kenneth Andrade, Head –

Investment, IDFC Asset Management; Leo Puri, Managing Director, UTI Asset Management Company (P) Ltd; Himanshu Kohli, CEO, Client Associates; Amit Jeffrey, Asset Allocation Manager, Client Associates; Rajeev Patel, food activist and author of *Stuffed and Starved*; Chirag Mehta, Senior Fund Manager – Alternative Investments, Quantum Asset Management Ltd; Satyajit Das, former investment banker and author of *Extreme Money*; Swati Kulkarni, Executive Vice President and Fund Manager – Equities, UTI Asset Management Company (P) Ltd; Rajesh Krishnan, CEO, Brick Eagle Investments; Om Ahuja, CEO, Jones Lang LaSalle India; Michael Donnan, Asia Pacific Art Director, Collin & Kent International; Dinesh Vazirani, founder, Saffronart; Deborah Yang, Managing Director and Head of the MSCI Index, EMEA, Morgan Stanley Capital International; Douglas Clayton, CEO, Leopard Capital; Hemindra Hazari; Rajeev Malik, senior economist at CLSA; Meera Sanyal, former CEO and Chairman, Royal Bank of Scotland, India; Rikesh Mirchandani, CEO, Ocean City Capital Advisors; Lalita D. Gupte, Non-executive Chairperson, ICICI Venture Funds Management Co. Ltd, and Chairperson, India Infradebt Limited; and Veena Mankar, Founder, Swadhaar Group.

To Avni Puri and Nish Bhutani, Alicia Torres, Himanshu Kohli and Deborah Yang, thanks for helping us with introductions.

To our agent, Priya Doraswamy, thank you for listening, offering advice and supporting us through this entire process.

To Poulomi Chatterjee, thanks for choosing to bring this book to the women of India and for offering all the painstaking editing advice over the course of the last year.

To Saumya Gaur, thank you for your help with research and editing.

And, above all else, a very special thank you to you, the women of India, for taking a definitive step towards becoming financially independent rather than relying upon your father, husband or son.